HANDS FREE
BUSINESS FRENCH

100 Essential French Business Phrases for English Speakers

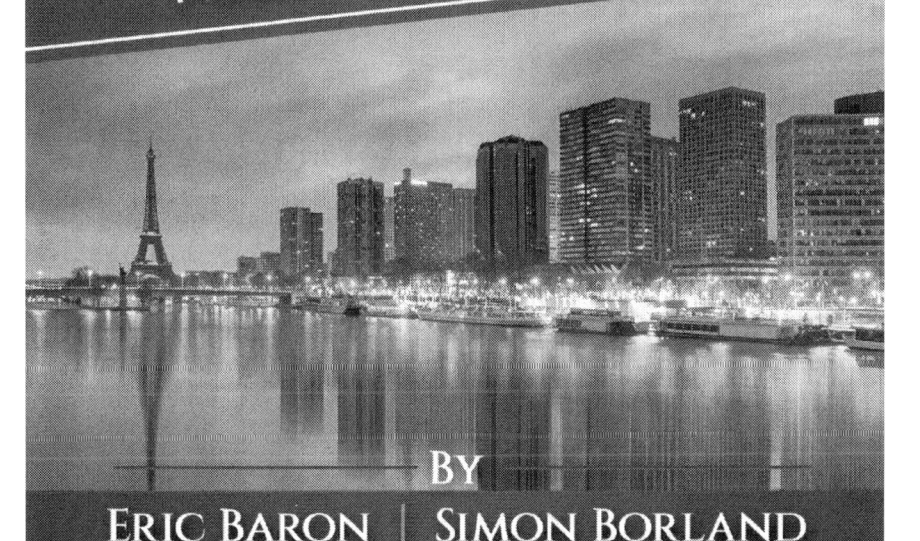

BY
ERIC BARON | SIMON BORLAND

Hands Free Business French
100
Essential Business French phrases
for English speakers

Also available as an audiobook. Download it on bit.ly/businessfrenchbook or scan this QR code:

Written by
Eric Baron and Simon Borland
Narrated by Eric Baron

Copyright © Eric Baron and Simon Borland 2018

HOW TO USE THIS BOOK

Welcome to Hands Free Business French by Eric Baron and Simon Borland.

This book is intended to help you learn the essential words and phrases to help you understand and express yourself in French business environments.

It is intended to be listened to as an audio book as well as read in print - the combined learning experience will be much faster for you if you use both. They are complementary but not identical. You can download it on or scan this QR code:

The first three chapters are a fast and clear introduction to French basics (conjugation rules and conversation starters).

The main body then starts at chapter 4, up to chapter 73, with the following structure for each chapter: one new French word/phrase, an example sentence to illustrate it, and a breakdown of each of the sentence's components.

The book ends with 6 extra chapters that are meant to hone your knowledge of Business French, with common expressions, false friends and specific vocabulary.

The book is filled with conjugation tables that are easily recognizable so you can flip through the book to find them.

English-French translations are also easy to find since every new word will be inside inverted commas, with the following format: 'English word' = « French word ».

You should also notice typography rules differ: punctuation, spacing, capitalisation and formatting are different from one language to the other. We strongly recommend you pay attention and replicate them in your written correspondence.

Bon courage !

Table of Contents

Introduction 1
1. Basic conjugation 3
2. Sentence Starters 7
3. Basic conversation 9
4. "to send": « envoyer » 12
5. "an increase": « une augmentation » 15
6. "to drop": « baisser » 18
7. "operations": « les opérations » 21
8. "a salesman": « un commercial » 22
9. "a trend": « une tendance » 24
10. "the figures": "les chiffres" 25
11. "a record": « des notes » 26
12. "the brand": « la marque » 27
13. "a factory": « une usine » 29
14. "the warehouse": « le magasin » 31
15. "the depot": « l'entrepôt » 33
16. "the production": « la production » 36
17. "a project": « un projet » 38
18. "a pie chart": « un diagramme en secteurs » 40
19. "a conference call": « une conf call » 42
20. "the closing date": « la date limite » 44
21. "industrial process": « le processus industriel » 46
22. "customer relations": « le service client » 50

23.	"a fault" : « une faute »	52
24.	"a delivery" : « une livraison »	55
25.	"a concern" : « un sujet de préoccupation »	57
26.	"to turn" : « transformer »	59
27.	"responsible" : « responsable »	61
28.	"a department" : « une direction »	63
29.	"Lean" : « le Lean »	65
30.	"a downsizing" : « une réduction d'effectifs »	66
31.	"cost-cutting" : « réduction des coûts »	68
32.	"a product" : « un produit »	71
33.	"a mixed picture" : « une situation mitigée »	72
34.	"successful" : « être un succès »	76
35.	"the purpose" : « l'objectif »	78
36.	"the vacancies" : « les postes vacants »	79
37.	"to argue" : « se disputer »	81
38.	"the research" : « la recherche »	84
39.	"an advertisement" : « une annonce »	86
40.	"a team" : « un service »	87
41.	"an application" : « une candidature »	90
42.	"an interview" : « un entretien »	92
43.	"an update" : « un point »	95
44.	"the market share" : « la part de marché »	96
45.	"the supply chain" : « la supply chain »	98
46.	"a rise" : « une augmentation »	101
47.	"to achieve" : « atteindre »	103
48.	"the performance" : « la performance »	105
49.	"a campaign" : « une campagne »	107

50. "the capital": « le capital » 110
51. "customer data": « les données clients » 112
52. "a database": « une base de données » 114
53. "the earnings": « les revenus » 116
54. "a deposit": « un dépôt » 118
55. "an engagement": « un rendez-vous » 120
56. "to fill out": « REMPLIR » 122
57. "innovation": « l'innovation » 124
58. "internal": « interne » 126
59. "managerial": « managérial » 127
60. "the opening hours": « les horaires d'ouvertures » 128
61. "to pick up someone": « aller chercher quelqu'un » .. 129
62. "a quote": « un devis » 131
63. "a brick and mortar shop": « un point de vente » 132
64. "to run out": « ne plus avoir de » 134
65. "to state": « formuler » 136
66. "to carry out": « mener à bien » 138
67. "a workshop": « un atelier » 140
68. "a wage": « un salaire » 142
69. "accommodation": « un logement » 144
70. "mergers/acquisitions": « les fusions acquisitions » . 146
71. "bankrupt": « en faillite » 148
72. "root cause": « une cause racine » 150
73. "a day off": « un jour de congé » 152
74. False friends 154
75. Software vocabulary..155
76. Private banking 158

77.	Career and positions	160
78.	Acronyms	162
79.	Sayings and metaphors	163
Final Words		165

Introduction

Bonjour, je m'appelle Eric Baron.

Hello, this is Eric Baron, and welcome to Hands Free Business French.

I'm a professional corporate translator and language coach, and today I'll be helping you fast-track your learning of Business French.

So many of my clients ask me the same question: "Eric, how can I learn Business French more quickly, so that I can operate more confidently in a business environment?"

Well, here is my answer.

I have put together this extensive audio programme for this exact purpose.

This is based on up-to-date phrases, jargon and parlance of French Business life - including some slang and tips to communicate better with locals, in a nuanced manner.

My system relies on a careful construction of business-related sentences, with increasing complexity. In every chapter, I will introduce a new noun or verb, give an example sentence, translate into in French, and then break the sentence down into each of its components.

Many chapters also include quick tips to add some nuance to your speech, and grammar points to explain core grammar notions, such as how to conjugate a verb, or how to use a specific tense.

There will be plenty of repetition from previous chapters as well.

Hearing each sentence from a native French speaker like myself, two or three times, is so important to my clients' accelerated learning, and that is also my preferred approach.

I don't want you to have to pause and rewind a chapter - I'd rather you hear it two or three times from me, as you listen.

Now, this audiobook assumes that you have some basic knowledge of French already. If you know what the European Framework for Languages is, you need at least a B1 level to make the most out of it. This means you're able to understand and participate in most everyday conversations, but you need to perfect your knowledge of Business French.

For those of you who find that you need a refresher in beginners French, make sure you check out my beginners audiobooks.

A final note - if you find yourself in a really tight spot and need urgent Business French help with translation, specifically legal documents or technical documents, or Business French coaching - please contact me directly.

This is my area of specialty, and I work with clients at every level of the business, up to board level, to accelerate their mastery and comprehension of Business French.

I operate on same-day translations for board level and urgent contractual documents worldwide.

Here is what I recommend: listen to this audiobook every day for about 30 minutes, when commuting, then when you get back home, read the matching part of the book. This will help you tremendously fast-track your learning.

1. Basic conjugation

This is a quick overview.

French verbs are conventionally divided into three conjugations, « conjugaisons » with the following grouping:

First group

You've got all the verbs ending in « -ER ». It's about 60% of them, except « ALLER » which belongs to the third.

Second group

You've got all the endings in « -IR » with the gerund ending in « -issant ». It's about 30% of all French verbs.

Third group

You've got all the rest. So, the first section is all the verbs ending in « -IR » but with their gerund ending in « -ant ». And the second section comprises the verbs ending with all the other endings like « -OIR », « -RE ». It's about 10% of all French verbs.

Like in English, there are regular and irregular verbs. The regular ones are easy to conjugate because you're just using the standard endings, depending on which group the verb belongs to. And then you've got the irregular verbs, which tend to be the most frequently used. They use the same endings but twist them slightly.

For example, in English a regular verb is "TO ACCEPT": accept, accepted, accepted (present, preterit, past participle).

An irregular verb would be "TO BLOW": blow, blew, blown.

In French a regular verb, a typical one is « MANGER »: "TO EAT". It ends in « -ER » so it belongs to the first group.

An irregular verb would be « AVOIR »: "TO HAVE", « ALLER »: "TO GO", « FAIRE »: "TO DO"/"TO MAKE", and « ETRE »: "TO BE".

With verbs, you must master the conjugations of the 6 persons in the present tense.

After that, you can very easily master the future, past and passé composé.

So here is an ultra-fast summary of some of the conjugation examples from each of the three groups.

First group

MARCHER – TO WALK (present)

Je march-e	I walk
Tu march-es	You walk
Il/Elle march-e	He/She walks
Nous march-ons	We walk
Vous march-ez	You walk
Ils/Elles march-ent	They walk

Second group

FINIR – TO END/TO FINISH (present)

Je fin-is	I finish
Tu fin-is	You finish
Il/Elle fin-it	He/She finishes
Nous fin-issons	We finish
Vous fin-issez	You finish
Ils/Elles fin-issent	They finish

Third group
DIRE – TO SAY (present)

Je di-s	I say
Tu di-s	You say
Il/Elle di-t	He/She says
Nous dis-ons	We say
Vous *dit-es*	You say
Ils/Elles dis-ent	They say

Watch out! « Vous *dites* » is highly irregular.

The three most important verbs

Now let's conjugate very irregular but very important verbs.

AVOIR (TO HAVE)

ETRE (TO BE)

ALLER (TO GO)

AVOIR – TO HAVE (present)

J'ai	I have
Tu as	You have
Il/Elle a	He/She has
Nous avons	We have
Vous avez	You have
Ils/Elles ont	They have

ETRE – TO BE (present)

Je suis	I am
Tu es	You are

Il/Elle est	He/She is
Nous sommes	We are
Vous êtes	You are
Ils/Elles sont	They are

ALLER – TO GO (present)

Je vais	I go
Tu vas	You go
Il/Elle va	He/She goes
Nous allons	We go
Vous allez	You go
Ils/Elles vont	They go

It's very important that you learn at least those three verbs by heart, the irregular ones and the regular ones with their endings, in the present tense.

Next we will refresh you on some very important sentence starters that you can use in any environment for any purpose.

2. Sentence Starters

We're going to learn some sentence starters that are useful in any environment to get the conversation going. These can be used in a non-business environment too.

SENTENCE STARTERS

Excuse me	Excusez-moi
Can I?	Puis-je ?
I would like	Je voudrais
I think that	Je pense que
Is it that?	Est-ce que ?
What is it that ?	Qu'est-ce que ?
In my opinion	A mon avis
Who?	Qui ?
What?	Que ?
Why?	Pourquoi ?
What is?/Which is?	Quel est ?
Here	Ici
There	Là-bas
Alright	D'accord
Please	S'il vous plaît
Today	Aujourd'hui
Yesterday	Hier
Tomorrow	Demain
Now	Maintenant
After	Après

Before	Avant
In front of	En face de
Next to	A côté de
How much is it?	Combien c'est/Combien ça coûte ?

Next, we are going to see some logical connectives i.e. words that are used to connect two sentences together.

LOGICAL CONNECTIVES

However	Cependant
For	Pour
So that	Afin de
And	Et
Or	Ou
But	Mais
If	Si

In the next chapter, we're going to see some conversation starters in a business environment.

3. Basic conversation

We're going to see some basic conversation starters that are really useful, especially in a business environment:

- How to introduce yourself
- How to talk about your position in your company
- How to talk about your level in French
- How to talk about your objectives for a seminar
- How to communicate with you in French

So, let's see first how to introduce yourself.

« Bonjour ! Je m'appelle Eric, j'ai trente ans, je suis américain, je viens de New York et je participe au séminaire ici à Paris. »

So, this means: "Hello! My name is Eric, I'm thirty, I'm American I come from New York and I'm taking part in the seminar here in Paris."

Let's tweak it a little bit for our UK friends:

« Bonjour ! Je m'appelle Eric, j'ai trente ans, je suis britannique, je viens de Londres et je participe au séminaire ici à Paris. »

So, this means, "Hello! My name is Eric, I'm thirty, I'm British, I come from London and I'm taking part in a seminar here in Paris."

Now let's talk about your position in your company.

« Je suis analyste marketing, je dirige une équipe de trois personnes. Mon chef est le directeur marketing pour l'Europe. Mon entreprise fournit des services de consulting en informatique. »

So, this means, "I'm a marketing analyst, I lead a team of three. My boss is the marketing director for Europe. My company offers IT consulting services."

Now let's talk about your level in French.

How to say "basic", "intermediate", "advanced", "expert".

"basic" is « débutant », as in « Je suis débutant » : "I have a basic level".

"intermediate" is just « intermédiaire »

« J'ai un niveau intermédiaire » : "I've got an intermediate level"

"advanced" is « avancé »

« J'ai un niveau avancé » : "I have an advanced level"

And finally, "expert" is « expert »

« J'ai un niveau expert » : "I have an expert level"

If you want to say for example, "I speak a bit of French but I'm not fluent. Please speak slowly and articulate.", you will say:

« Je parle un peu français mais je ne le parle pas couramment. Parlez lentement et en articulant s'il vous plaît. »

Now let's talk about your objectives for, say, a seminar.

If you want to say "I'm here at the seminar to meet my French colleagues and improve the communication between our two teams," you will say:

« Je participe au séminaire pour rencontrer mes collègues français et améliorer la communication entre nos deux services. »

Now let's see some quick tips on how to say please communicate with me in French this or that way.

"I may ask you to repeat.": « Je vais peut-être vous demander de répéter. »

"Please repeat": « Répétez s'il vous plaît »

"Can you please send me the seminar program or the meeting slides in advance?":

« Pouvez-vous m'envoyer le programme du séminaire ou les slides de la réunion à l'avance ? »

This is very useful because for every language you read better than you speak.

You should ask for any documents to be sent to you by email along with text exchanges over phone calls, which are harder to understand. So, if you want to say "Please favour written exchanges by e-mail or text to phone calls which are harder to understand for me.", you will say:

« Préférez s'il vous plaît les échanges écrits par e-mail ou texto aux appels téléphoniques qui sont plus difficiles à comprendre pour moi. »

This marks the end of the starter chapters.

Now we move on to the **100 business phrases.**

4. "to send": « envoyer »

Example sentence

"I send an email to the employees at 4 pm."

« J'envoie un email aux salariés à 4 heures. »

Let's hear it again.

« J'envoie un email aux salariés à 4 heures. »

Now let's break down the sentence.

"I send" is « j'envoie ».

The infinitive is « ENVOYER », it ends with « -ER ».

So, it's a first group verb like we discussed in the starter chapter. It conjugates very easily.

ENVOYER – TO SEND (present)

J'envoi-e	I send
Tu envoi-es	You send
Il/Elle envoi-e	He/She sends
Nous envoy-ons	We send
Vous envoy-ez	You send
Ils/Elles envoi-ent	They send

- Next, we have "an email": simply « un email ».

It's the same word because the French likes to borrow many English words, especially in business. But be careful with the pronunciation:

"an <u>e</u>mail" but « un e<u>mail</u> »: the French will almost always stress the last syllable.

- Next, we have "to the employees": « aux employés ».

« aux » is the contraction of « a + les ». It becomes one word, « aux »: "to the". Also, when I say « aux employés », be careful. Enhance the sound of the "S-link" [also called a liaison]: « aux-employés ».

- Then we have "at 4 pm": « à 4 (quatre) heures ».

In English you use "at 4 pm" because it's not ambiguous. If it's ambiguous, you use the 24-hour clock or the military clock, so 16:00. We do that in French as well. « 4 (quatre) heures » is not ambiguous.

If it was, say 8, it could be 8 am or 8 pm, we will say « 8 heures du matin »/« 8 heures du soir »: "8 am"/"8 pm" ; or using the military clock, « 8 (huit) heures »: « 20 (vingt) heures ».

Quick tip: "ASAP"

After most sentences, I will tell you a bit about key words, phrases or slang that's used in business French.

Here is our first one:

"ASAP", how do you say this? You can say « ASAP », the English word with a French pronunciation, or you can say « tout de suite », which means "immediately".

Quick tip 2: "A company-wide email"

How do you say "CC company wide" or "All" when you send an email to the entire company? You use « un all-staff », which means "a company wide email" - « un all-staff », with the N-liaison.

Grammar point: « PARLER »

Now as shown in the starter chapter before this, we're going to do some grammar points.

Let's do a quick conjugation of this new verb « PARLER ».

« PARLER »: "TO SPEAK" is a first group verb. So:

PARLER – TO SPEAK (present)

Je parl-e	I speak
Tu parl-es	You speak
Il/Elle parl-e	He/She speaks
Nous parl-ons	We speak
Vous parl-ez	You speak
Ils/Elles parl-ent	They speak

Be careful: the third person and the sixth person often sound the same, even though they are spelled differently.

You noticed that « PARLER »: "TO SPEAK" conjugates just like « ENVOYER », which we just did at the beginning of the chapter. That's because they're both first group verbs and they are very regular. So, you only need to learn the endings and then you remove « -ER », and you add the regular endings.

Ok that's a lot we have already covered.

Here is the full sentence again:

"I send an email to the employees at 4 pm."

« J'envoie un email aux salariés à 4 heures. »

5. "an increase": « une augmentation »

Example sentence

"I ask the director for an increase in the marketing budget."

« *Je demande au directeur une augmentation du budget marketing.* »

Breakdown

- "I ask": « je demande »

« je demande » is the first person of « DEMANDER »: "TO ASK".

It ends with « -ER », first group, easy.

Let's conjugate it:

DEMANDER – TO ASK (present)

Je demand-e	I ask
Tu demand-es	You ask
Il/Elle demand-e	He/She asks
Nous demand-ons	We ask
Vous demand-ez	You ask
Ils/Elles demand-ent	They ask

- "to the director"/"the director": « le directeur »

Why do we have an English "I ask the director", but in French it's not « je demande le directeur », it's « je demande au directeur »?

Well, verbs are used differently in English and in French. In English, "to ask" is transitive direct here. So, you only need to place the object of the action right after the verb. But in

French you will need a little something, a preposition like "to": « à ». « DEMANDER » is transitive indirect. So, you will use « je demande à le directeur » but it's ugly, so we contract it into « au »: « je demande au directeur ».

- "an increase": « une augmentation »

"TO INCREASE" would be « AUGMENTER », « -ER », first group.

- "in the marketing budget": « du budget marketing »

You see that we use different prepositions, "in": « du ».

« du » is not "in". « du » is "of the".

It's like saying "I asked the director for an increase of the marketing budget."

Like often, English and French will use words that are not exact equivalents, so you need to understand how each language works.

Quick tip: Latin-derived synonyms

"the director": « le directeur »

See how similar it is. When you're struggling, think of a Latin-derived synonym in English. There's a very high chance it will be the same, it will be transparent in French.

Grammar point: Genders

Genders in French are very hard to remember. Most of them are just random, there's no logic behind. So you have to use your memory. Don't worry, there are a few rules like trees, seasons, days of the week, months.

For example, months and seasons are always masculine.

You also have masculine and feminine endings.

For example, words that end with « -ement » are always masculine. [Note: the audio doesn't make any distinction between « -ement » and the other endings].

Words that end with « -ssion »/« -ude »/« -sion »/« -ade » are always feminine.

e.g. Masculine: « l'engagement »: "engagement"

e.g. Feminine: « la fortitude »: "fortitude", « la passion »: "passion".

6. "to drop": « baisser »

Example sentence

"Sales dropped in Q1."

« Les ventes ont baissé en T1. »

Breakdown

- "sales": « les ventes »
- "TO DROP": « BAISSER »

"to drop" literally means to fall down. But English uses very practical images whereas French is more theoretical. « BAISSER » is "TO DECREASE".

- "in Q1": « en T1 » (pronounced « té-un »)

So, Q1 means "the first quarter," « T1 » means « le premier trimestre ».

In English you have two words, "quarter" and "trimester". These mean the same thing in different contexts. In French, there's only one word: « un trimestre ».

Quick tip: Articles

You see that "sales" has no article in English but « les ventes » has an article in French.

Here is a golden rule for you. You always need an article in French. There are few exceptions. When in doubt, use an article, either a definite article like here « les ventes »: "the sales" or an indefinite article like « des ventes »: "some sales".

Grammar point: Le passé composé

That is a very useful tense in the past. Why is it used? It is the standard past tense. It describes a past event that influences the present and is now complete. It describes a brief event, not a continuous background event.

For example:

"Sales have dropped suddenly": « Les ventes ont baissé d'un coup ».

versus

"Sales were dropping steadily throughout Q1": « Les ventes baissaient régulièrement au cours du T1 ».

So, in the first sentence "have dropped": « ont baissé », I used « passé composé » (brief event).

In the second sentence: "were dropping": « baissaient », I used « imparfait » which is a different past, a continuous background event past.

How does it work? You use the auxiliary verb, l'auxiliaire « ETRE »: "TO BE" or « AVOIR »: "TO HAVE", in the present, and then you add the past participle [Note: the audio incorrectly says "principle"] of the main verb.

For example:

"have dropped": « ont baissé »

« ont » is the verb « AVOIR » in the present, and « baissé » is the past participle of the verb « BAISSER » (infinitive). So, you have six declensions for « BAISSER ».

Let's conjugate it in the « passé composé »:

BAISSER – TO DROP (present)

Je baiss-e	I drop
Tu baiss-es	You drop
Il/Elle baiss-e	He/She drops
Nous baiss-ons	We drop
Vous baiss-ez	You drop
Ils/Elles baiss-ent	They drop

You see, it is really easy because the past participle doesn't change, only « AVOIR » changes because it's conjugated in the present.

Let's now conjugate a third group « PRENDRE »: "TO TAKE". « PRENDRE » ends with « -RE », so it rightly belongs to the third group.

PRENDRE – TO TAKE (present)

Je pren-ds	I take
Tu pren-ds	You take
Il/Elle pren-d	He/She takes
Nous pren-ons	We take
Vous pren-ez	You take
Ils/Elles prenn-ent	They take

So, you see that it works exactly the same. « AVOIR » is conjugated in the present, to which you add the past participle of « PRENDRE », which is « pris ».

7. "operations": « les opérations »

Example sentence

"The operations department is huge."

« La direction des opérations est énorme. »

Breakdown

- "the department": « la direction »

False friend alert!

"the department" is not « le département ». Typically, in French, « un département » is a territorial division of the French country and « la direction » is not always "the direction". Be very careful of these false friends. Every time we come across a false friend, I will have this false friend alert for you.

- "the operations department": « la direction des opérations ».

See how the syntax is different in French. In English, you may just turn a noun into an adjective by placing it before the other noun. So, you've got the main noun which is "department", and the side noun which is "operations". "operations" is like an adjective, "the operations department": "the department of operations".

In French you can't do that. You have to use « de » or « des », which means "of".

So « la direction des operations »: main noun + « de »/« des » + side noun.

- "is huge": « est énorme ».

Be careful, there is a T-link when you pronounce it (« est‿énorme »). Likewise, when you say « des opérations », you have an S-link (pronounced « lez‿opérations »).

8. "a salesman": « un commercial »

Example sentence

"I ask the salesman to show the products."

« Je demande au commercial de montrer les produits. »

Breakdown

- "a salesman": « un commercial »

Note that it in this context, you have to use « un commercial ».

It's not just someone who sells, it's not « un vendeur ». That would be "a shop assistant" or a "retail assistant".

With "I ask a salesman to show the products," it's « un commercial », it's a higher position.

- "to show": « de MONTRER »

Notice that the syntax is different again, "I ask the salesman", but in French you have to use a preposition: « Je demande au commercial ».

- "the products": « les produits »

Quick tip: "TO SHOW"

Again, if you're struggling to find the correct word or the correct translation in French, think of a Latin-derived synonym in English. "TO SHOW" is like "TO DEMONSTRATE": « MONTRER/DÉMONTRER ».

Grammar point: "TO ASK" vs « DEMANDER »

"to show" was translated as « de montrer ». Why is that?

Well "ask **to** show" is how the verb "ask" works in English, but in French « demander **de** montrer » is how the verb works in French.

So again, keep in mind that the prepositions that are placed after verbs are often different in both languages.

Let's conjugate it:

« MONTRER », « -ER », first group. So, we remove « -ER », we've got the root « montr- » and we add the regular first group endings:

MONTRER – TO SHOW (present)

Je montr-e	I show
Tu montr-es	You show
Il/Elle montr-e	He/She shows
Nous montr-ons	We show
Vous montr-ez	You show
Ils/Elles montr-ent	They show

9. "a trend": « une tendance »

Example sentence

"The consumer trends are different in Paris."

« Les tendances de consommation sont différentes à Paris. »

Breakdown

- "a consumer": « un consommateur ». The female version is « une consommatrice »
- "a consumer trend": « une tendance de consommation »

Again, the English says noun + noun. The French says noun + « de » + noun: « une tendance de consommation ».

- "different": « différentes ».

Make sure you match the gender and number of the noun with the gender and number of the matching adjective. So, in this case, "different" applies to "consumer trends". In « tendances de consommation », the main noun is « tendance », and it is feminine plural, so « différentes » needs to be feminine plural.

10. "the figures": "les chiffres"

Example sentence

"The figures are bad this quarter, again."

« Les chiffres sont de nouveau mauvais ce trimestre. »

Breakdown

- "the figures": "les chiffres"

Remember in Casino Royale, the villain was called « Le Chiffre » because he's good with numbers. Well that's it! « le chiffre » is "a digit", « les chiffres »: the "the figures".

- "the quarter": « le trimestre »
- "bad": « mauvais »

Again, as with all adjectives in French, don't forget to match their gender and number with the gender number of the matching noun. « les chiffres » is masculine plural, so « mauvais » needs to be masculine plural. The feminine plural version would be « mauvaises ».

- "again": « de nouveau »/« à nouveau »

Quick tip: Order of words

The order of words matters. When you say "the figures are bad this quarter **again**" you add something, you enhance an emotion like anger, "again". You can also do this in French, but it will be rarer and stronger.

If you put it at the end, it becomes extremely emphasised.

e.g. « Les chiffres sont mauvais ce trimestre, **à nouveau**. » (written version)

« Les chiffres sont mauvais ce trimestre, **encore une fois**. » (oral version)

11. "a record": « des notes »

Example sentence

"I made a record of our meeting."

« J'ai pris des notes sur notre réunion. »

Breakdown

- "I made": « j'ai pris »

So that's "TO TAKE": « PRENDRE », in the passé composé, the standard past tense.

"TO MAKE" is usually « FAIRE », but it's a set phrase, it's a different expression here.

So, you're not going to say « j'ai fait des notes », you will say "I have taken notes": « j'ai pris des notes ».

- "a meeting": « une réunion »

You may say « un meeting » because in business French, you will borrow a lot of English words.

- "our": « notre »

It's a possessive pronoun. You need to learn all 6 of the possessive pronouns and their different variations, it's very important.

Quick tip: "To take notes"

How do you say to take notes?

Well it's the exact same French expression.

"to make a record" or "to take notes" is going to be « prendre des notes ».

This is going to happen a lot, sometimes you have several expressions in English and only one good translation in French. Sometimes it's the other way around.

12. "the brand": « la marque »

Example sentence

"The designers create the packaging for the brand."

« Les designers créent le packaging pour la marque. »

Breakdown

- "a designer": « un designer »

That's another example of a borrowed word. This is very frequent in marketing and sales. Be careful, the pronunciation is different: "a de<u>si</u>gner": « un designe<u>r</u> ». Stress the last syllable in French.

- "TO CREATE": « CRÉER »

Let's conjugate it. « CRÉER », « -ER », first group, simple, regular.

CRÉER – TO CREATE (present)

Je cré-e	I create
Tu cré-es	You create
Il/Elle cré-e	He/She creates
Nous cré-ons	We create
Vous cré-ez	You create
Ils/Elles cré-ent	They create

Reminder: « il crée » (third person he/she), and « ils créent » (sixth person, they) are pronounced the same but they are spelled differently.

- "the packaging": « le packaging »

Another example of a borrowed word.

- "for the brand": « pour la marque »

"for" is usually translated as « pour », as the objective/the goal.

"the brand" is just « la marque ».

When you mention branding as a marketing concept, you can just say « le branding ».

Another example of a borrowed word with a different pronunciation.

Quick tip: Silent letters

A quick note on silent letters, such as in « créent » (sixth person): it's very important that you keep them silent, but you know exactly how to spell the word. Silent letters are very common in French, in final letters and in diphthongs. A diphthong is one sound that is created by adding several letters together. It exists in English and in French.

For example, a diphthong in English would be "ding dong": it creates two new sounds. Adding "in" and "on" before the "g" creates two new sounds, "-ing" and "-ong".

Back to silent letters, there is no golden rule in French to memorize, but there are patterns that you can memorize.

For example, the sixth person in many conjugated verbs is going to be like that, with silent « -nt » at the end.

For example, in « MARCHER »: "TO WORK", the third person is « il marche » and the sixth person is « ils marchent », with the same pronunciation.

13. "a factory": « une usine »

Example sentence
"There is a factory near the train station."
« Il y a une usine près de la gare. »

Breakdown
- "there is": « il y a »
- « il » is the third person, like "it" (neutral).
- « y » is like "there". « y » can be "here" or "there" when it's contracted

The normal form is « là », e.g. « on va là »: "we go there".

If you place it before, « on y va », « là » becomes « y ».

This doesn't happen in English. In "we go there", "there" never changes; "there we go"/"we go there".

- « a » is the third person, present tense of « AVOIR »

So, it's like "there it is".

- "near": « près de »

That's another example of different prepositions. "near" is just one word but we need both « près de » in French, not to mention the article « la » in « la gare ».

« près de la gare »: "near the train station".

- "the train station" is just « la gare ».

Usually the English is more concise but there are exceptions like this one.

We don't say « la gare de train », it's implicit.

If you visit Paris by train from London, say, you'll be familiar with « la Gare du Nord », "the Nothern train station". This is where you will get off when you take the Eurostar train and it's also where you will go to visit « le Sacré-Cœur », the big white basilica.

Quick tip: How to buy tickets

If you want to ask for tickets here's what you do:

- « Je voudrais acheter un billet aller-retour »: "I would like to buy a return ticket"
- "a one-way ticket" is « un aller simple ».

Quick tip: "a factory"

You can also say "a plant" for "a factory" in English.

But there's only one good word in French and that's « une usine ».

You may say "a production site": « un site the production ».

"a business unit" is the same: « une business unit ». It's a borrowed word.

Grammar point: « il y a »

In English, "there is"/"there are" are used depending on whether it's singular or plural, but in French there's only one phrase, « il y a », which never changes.

14. "the warehouse": « le magasin »

Example sentence

"The warehouse is the place where supplies are found."

« Le magasin est l'endroit où les approvisionnements se trouvent. »

Breakdown

- "the place": « l'endroit »
- "where": « où », with an accent. (Note that « ou » with no accent means "or")
- « le magasin » can also mean "the shop". Here in the context of a factory, it means "the warehouse"
- "supplies": « les approvisionnements »

Remember, you always need an article in French, even if it's not present in English, e.g. "supplies": « les approvisionnements ».

You may shorten it to « appro »/« les appros », that's colloquial, everyone understands this in a factory.

"the procurement department" is also called « les appros »/« les approvisionnements ».

- "are found": « se trouvent », from the verb « SE TROUVER » which comes from « TROUVER »: "TO FIND".

Grammar point: Pronominal verbs

This is a pronominal verb in French. So, in English we have "are found" which is just the passive voice of "TO FIND" and it's translated as the pronominal verb « SE TROUVER ».

So, what's a pronominal verb or pronominal form? The pronominal form of a verb is when the subject of the action and the object of the action is the same person.

For example, in English "I wash myself": « je me lave ».

"I" is doing the action and "I" is also receiving the action of washing.

So, this is the case here in French, in the French translation only: « se trouvent ».

SE TROUVER – TO FIND ONESELF (present)

Je me trouv-e	I find myself
Tu te trouv-es	You find yourself
Il/Elle se trouv-e	He/She finds him/herself
Nous nous trouv-ons	We find ourselves
Vous vous trouv-ez	You find yourselves
Ils/Elles se trouv-ent	They find themselves

15. "the depot": « l'entrepôt »

Example sentence

"The depot is where final products are stored."

« L'entrepôt est l'endroit où les produits finis sont stockés. »

Breakdown

- "the depot": « l'entrepôt »

Again, we're in the context of a factory.

So, we've seen the other end, "the warehouse": « le magasin », and now "the depot": « l'entrepôt ».

- "is where": « est l'endroit où »

You noticed that the French needs to add « l'endroit »: "the place where".

The English doesn't have to do this, and English prepositions are more meaningful.

"Where" is enough to say that it's "the place where". But the French needs to add « l'endroit où ».

- "final products": « les produits finis »

The French literally says "finished products" and not "final", so be careful.

- "TO STORE": « STOCKER »

Again, that's a borrowed English word: "stock".

You may use a synonym which is more French, « RANGER ».

But in the context of the factory/a company, « STOCKER » is more common.

« RANGER » is also when you tidy up your room.

"the stocks": « les inventaires »

What is "input" and "output"? Well, the translation depends on the context.

In electronics you will say « entrée »/« sortie. »

« entrée » is "input" (think of "entrance"); « sortie » is "output" (think of "exit").

In the context of the factory, "input" and "output" are actually « approvisionnements » and « produits », as we've seen.

So, every translation is very contextual. My clients often ask me why I translate this word that way because they thought the translation was actually a different word. Well it's not that simple. A word is very rarely equivalent to another word. In most cases a translation will depend on the context, on what you've just said, on the specificities of each language.

So, you see that in the context of electronics and in the context of a factory, the translation in French will be entirely different.

Grammar point: The passive voice

Again, you need to match the gender and number of each adjective and past participle with the gender and number of the noun.

Here, the past participle acts as an adjective. For example "final products are stored".

There is no problem in English, it's going to be "stored" whether it's masculine or feminine, singular or plural. But in the French « les produits finis sont stockés », « stockés » will vary.

Since « les produits finis » is a masculine plural noun, the past participle « stockés » will need to be masculine plural.

Usually the mark of the feminine will be an extra « -e » at the end of a word, and the mark of the plural will be an extra « -s ».

So that's why you have no extra « -e » and an extra « -s » in « stockés ».

Another example would be "taken". "TO TAKE", "taken". No problem in English.

With « PRENDRE », the past participle will be « pris ». « pris » is your masculine singular form.

If you need to make it feminine you will add an « -e »: « prise ».

If you need to make it plural you need to add an « -s »: « prises ».

16. "the production": « la production »

Example sentence

"The production is what the factory makes."

« La production est ce que l'usine fabrique. »

Breakdown

- "the factory": « l'usine »
- "TO MAKE": « FABRIQUER »

Quick tip: « FAIRE » vs « FABRIQUER »

What's the difference between « FAIRE » and « FABRIQUER »? Well it's about the same difference that you have in English with "TO DO" and "TO MAKE".

"TO DO" is more generic. "TO MAKE" is more practical. You've got a close equivalent of « FABRIQUER » with "TO FABRICATE". However, unlike "TO FABRICATE", « FABRIQUER » never means "TO MAKE UP" or "TO LIE".

Interesting fact

"TO FABRICATE" or « FABRIQUER » gave "manufacture" in both languages because it comes from the Latin "hand", so "manu-facture": "you fabricate with your hands".

Grammar point: Words ending in "-tion"

You need to have the « -tion » rule in mind.

Very often a "-tion" word in English will give a « -tion » word in French, and they will be very similar.

That's because we have shared Latin roots like in "manufacture", and it's also because we've had mutual influence ever since the Norman Conquest in 1066, e.g. "tuition", "intuition", "accumulation".

[Note: Both the French and English "-tion" nouns come from the fifth verbal form in Latin, called the "supine", e.g. accumulo, accumulare, accumulavi, accumulatus, **accumulatum**"].

"intuition" is « l'intuition », same word.

"accumulation" is « l'accumulation », same word.

But beware of some traps like "recognition". The translation is not ~~« récognition »~~ (this word does not exist).

- "recognition" is « la reconnaissance ».

17. "a project": « un projet »

Example sentence

"I finish each project on time."

« Je finis chaque projet à temps. »

Breakdown

- « je finis »: "I finish"

So, the infinitive is "TO FINISH": « FINIR ».

« FINIR » is a second group verb because it ends with « -IR », and its gerund ends with « -issant ».

Let's conjugate it:

FINIR – TO END/TO FINISH (present)

Je fin-is	I finish
Tu fin-is	You finish
Il/Elle fin-it	He/She finishes
Nous fin-issons	We finish
Vous fin-issez	You finish
Ils/Elles fin-issent	They finish

- "each": « chaque »

"each" and « chaque » are both invariable words, meaning they don't change whatever their form, singular or plural, masculine or feminine. We've seen that before. All English adjectives are invariable, which is very simple, but in French their gender and number need to be matched with the nouns.

- "on time": « à temps »

There's another expression in English which says "in time", and it's slightly different, but it's still « à temps » in French.

Quick tip: "TO TERMINATE"

"TO TERMINATE" as a synonym of "TO FINISH"

Be careful, false friend alert!

"TO TERMINATE" is not « TERMINER ». "TO TERMINATE" is to put an early end to something; "TO KILL" a contract, a project. That would be in French « RÉSILIER »: "TO RESILIATE".

- « TERMINER » is not "TO KILL", but "TO COMPLETE". It's neutral, not negative.

Grammar point: The present perfect in French

- "I finish": « je finis »

What about "I am finishing"? How do I say this?

Well you also say « je finis », because the present perfect does not exist in French, there's only one present.

So, if you really need to mention an ongoing action, you will use « en train de ».

"I am finishing the project": « Je suis en train de finir le projet ».

It's like the very old and formal English, "in train", meaning "underway", for example you could say an "an investigation is in train".

But in French, it's very normal and very frequent to say « en train », e.g. « Je suis en train de faire »: "I am doing".

18. "a pie chart": « un diagramme en secteurs »

Example sentence

"I think pie charts are hard to read."

« À mon avis, les diagrammes en secteurs sont difficiles à lire. »

Breakdown

- "a chart" is just « un graphique ». But if you add something, you specify which chart, like "a pie chart", it is going to be « un diagramme en secteurs »/« un diagramme en rectangles »
- "I think": « je pense que »

That is often implicit in English, but we always need « que » in French.

"I think"/"I think that": « je pense que ».

I used only « à mon avis » instead of « je pense que » for "I think", just to alternate between the expressions I'm using. You should do this too in a business context or in a social situation, switch it up to sound more knowledgeable.

Fun fact

"a pie chart" is also called « un camembert » in French.

This French cheese is the smelliest and the tastiest.

- "hard": « difficile »

« dur » is also a synonym, it works and it also has the physical meaning that "hard" has, like a "hard surface": « une surface dure ».

« difficile » only means challenging.

Quick tip: Order of circumstantial information

Circumstantial information can be moved around in English and in French. For example, "I think": « je pense » could be at the beginning or at the end. Be careful! I said « je pense », not « je pense que ».

You cannot place « je pense que » at the end, you can only place it at the beginning.

But you can place « je pense » at the end.

Circumstantial information that doesn't include a verb like "in my opinion": « à mon avis » can be placed anywhere in the sentence like in English - "in my opinion, pie charts are hard to read"/"pie charts are hard to read, in my opinion": « à mon avis les diagrammes en secteurs sont difficiles à lire »/« les diagrammes en secteurs sont difficiles à lire, à mon avis ».

19. "a conference call": « une conf call »

Example sentence

"Let's do a conference call about employee performance at noon."

« Faisons une conf call sur la performance des collaborateurs à midi. »

Breakdown

- "let's"/"let's do": « faisons »

The English is able to use a soft imperative using "let's" as in "let us do something/see something".

You're basically giving an order in a soft way.

There is no such soft imperative in French. So, you have to use the imperative mode to give an order or an instruction: « faisons » is the imperative mode for « FAIRE »: "TO DO". But we'll cover it later.

- "a conference call": « une conf call »

This is a very peculiar example of a borrowed word from the English, which was changed into a new word that doesn't even exist in English: « une conf call ».

Notice that it's feminine because « une conférence » is feminine.

- "employee performance": « la performance des collaborateurs ».

Note that « employé » or "employee" does exist but « collaborateur » is more politically correct.

It's because it seems like you're erasing the notion of hierarchy.

"to collaborate" is to work together so if you're "a collaborator": « un collaborateur », you're just part of a team.

- "at noon": « à midi »
- "TO DO": « FAIRE »

« FAIRE» belongs to the third group because its ending is « -RE ». So, what you do is as usual, you remove the ending, you remove « -RE » you get the root « fai- » and you add the regular or less regular endings of the third group.

FAIRE – TO DO (present)

Je fai-s	I do
Tu fai-s	You do
Il/Elle fai-t	He/She does
Nous fais-ons	We do
Vous *fait-es*	You do
Ils/Elles f-ont	They do

« vous *faites* » is very irregular. Keep in mind that this is a very common verb, so it is irregular.

One of the golden rules in all languages is that the more common the word, the more distorted it gets, because everyone uses it all the time.

20. "the closing date": « la date limite »

Example sentence

"You did not meet the deadline, that's unacceptable."

« Vous n'avez pas respecté la deadline, c'est inacceptable. »

Breakdown

- "the deadline": « la deadline »

Another example of a borrowed word. Alternative : la date limite.

- "to meet the deadline": « respecter la deadline »

Another example of a Latin-derived transparent word. The English may use "to respect the deadline", but it's less common.

- "unacceptable": « inacceptable »

Be careful with prefixes (the beginning of words) [Note: the audio mentions "affixes", which include both prefixes and suffixes]. They can be different from English to French.

In this case, "UN-acceptable" becomes « IN-acceptable ».

There are many other words like this, for example "unbearable": « insupportable ».

But sometimes it's the same affix, e.g. "inefficient": « inefficace ».

Also keep in mind the T-liaison when I pronounce « c'est-inacceptable ». That's because the first word ends with a "T" and the second word begins with a vowel. So, I need to make the T-liaison very clear: « c'est-inacceptable ».

Quick tip: Slang for "deadline"

You've got a slang word for "deadline" which is « dernier carat ». This is the last date, the last day, the last opportunity to do something.

Origin: back in the times, 24 carats was perfection for a jewel. It was the limit; hence the deadline.

So, you will say for example « mardi, c'est le dernier carat », meaning "Tuesday is the closing date/the deadline".

Quick tip 2: Formality

I said "you did not meet the deadline": « vous n'avez pas respecté la deadline ».

As you know, there are two levels of formality in French when addressing someone directly:

« tu », the second person, and « vous », the fifth person.

« tu » is for colleagues, friends and « vous » for your boss or the elders usually.

But this depends on the company you work in. For example, millenials and young bosses or young companies like Facebook will use « tu » all the time. But in a traditional company, a big multinational bank where you wear a suit and tie, you will address everyone with « vous ».

21. "industrial process": « le processus industriel »

Example sentence

"How can we improve our industrial process? Let's start with an assessment."

« Comment pouvons-nous améliorer notre processus industriel ? Commençons par un bilan. »

Breakdown

- "how?": « comment ? »

That's very standard. Most of the time, it is going to be translated as « comment ? ».

"CAN" is a modal verb in English. Modal verbs don't really exist in French. So, it is going to be rendered as « POUVOIR »: "TO BE ABLE TO".

Let's conjugate « POUVOIR », third group, the ending is « -OIR ». So, the root is « pouv- », but it's highly irregular. Let's conjugate it:

POUVOIR – TO BE ABLE (present)

Je peu-x	I am able
Tu peu-x	You are able
Il/Elle peu-t	He/She is able
Nous pouv-ons	We are able
Vous pouv-ez	You are able
Ils/Elles peuv-ent	They are able

- "we can": « nous pouvons »

In this case, it is a question so it is inverted: "can we?": « pouvons-nous ? »

- "TO IMPROVE": « AMÉLIORER »

First group verb, « AMÉLIORER ».

- "our...": « notre... »

Remember it is a possessive adjective [Note: the audio incorrectly says "pronoun"], so you need to learn them. Let's do all 6:

POSSESSIVE ADJECTIVES
(masculine/feminine/plural)

Mon/Ma/Mes	My
Ton/Ta/Tes	Your
Son/Sa/Ses	His/Her
Notre/Notre/Nos	Our
Votre/Votre/Vos	Your
Leur/Leur	Their

- "the industrial process": « le processus industriel ».

« industriel » is transparent and easy, it's the same word. But « processus » is not "process".

« process » also exists because, again, business French likes to borrow English words, but the real French word which comes from Latin, is « processus ». You can see the Latin root in the "-us" ending.

- "TO START": « COMMENCER »

First group, let's conjugate it:

COMMENCER – TO START (present)

| Je commenc-e | I start |

Tu commenc-es	You start
Il/Elle commenc-e	He/She starts
Nous commenç-ons	We start
Vous commenc-ez	You start
Ils/Elles commenc-ent	They start

- "an assessment": « un bilan »

Grammar point: How to make a question

How do you turn a statement into a question?

There are three different types of questions in French.

You can use an inversion like we did:

- « Comment pouvons-nous ? »
- « Es-tu libre vendredi ? »: "Are you free on Friday?"/ « Es-tu…? »= « Tu es…? »: "You are…?"= "Are you…?". Hence « Es-tu libre vendredi ? ».

This is the polite formal way of asking a question. If you have to write a question, you will use this.

You may also use the famous « Est-ce que ? »; which literally means "Is it that ?".

- « Est-ce que tu es libre vendredi ? »: "Is it that you are free on Friday?"

This is a standard question.

And the third way to do this is simply to express a statement with the same words and the same order, just changing your intonation at the end, like in English.

« Tu es libre vendredi ? »: "You free on Friday?"

It is much more common in French. Notice how I raise my voice at the very end. « Tu es libre vendredi ? ». That's the informal, colloquial, oral way of asking a question around friends and family.

22. "customer relations": « le service client »

Example sentence

"Customer relations are the first contact point of the company."

« Le service client est le premier point de contact de l'entreprise. »

Breakdown

- "a customer": « un client »
- "relations": « les relations »
- "customer relations....": « le service client »

It's a set phrase. It is how every department that manages customers is called.

- "Customer relations are": « Les relations clients sont »

Here « le service client » is singular, hence « est », third person of "TO BE": « ETRE ».

- "the first": « le premier »

You need to be careful, this is another adjective. It needs to have the same gender and number as « le service client ». « le service client » is masculine singular; « le premier » will be masculine singular too.

- "a contact point": « un point de contact ». Very similar.
- "the company": « l'entreprise »

We may use « la compagnie » for niche cases like « la compagnie pétrolière »: "the oil company", or "the gas company": « la compagnie de gaz », "the electricity company":

« la compagnie d'électricité ». But for all other companies, it's going to be « l'entreprise ».

Quick tip: "of"

What do you do with "of"? It's usually « de » e.g. "The Lord of the Rings": « Le Seigneur des anneaux ».

It is also used for possession. When the English says "my neighbour's dog", " 's " is typically English, so you have to find something else in French. So, you use « de ». "My neighbour's dog": « le chien de mon voisin ». It is called a genitive. When you are finding the origin, cause or owner of something, you need to use « de »: "of".

Grammar point: Plurals

You need to be very careful. Sometimes a plural English noun will be singular in French. Sometimes a singular in English will be plural in French, and you have to adapt your articles. For example, « de » is singular. If you use a plural, you have to use « des ».

e.g. « une entreprise »/« des entreprises »: "a company"/"some companies".

This is the indefinite article.

Even when you use "of" as « de », you also need to use « des » in the plural.

So, "my neighbour's dog"="the dog of my neighbour" (singular): « le chien de mon voisin ».

But "The Lord of the Rings" (plural): « Le Seigneur des anneaux ». And be careful because the final "s" will very often be silent at the end of the word. For example, « une entreprise », « des entreprises ». You can't hear it but the mark of the plural, the final "s", is there.

23. "a fault": « une faute »

Example sentence

"It's my fault we're late."

« C'est de ma faute si on est en retard. »

Breakdown

Let's hear some variants.

- "at fault": « une faute grave »

"Eric was at fault": « Eric a commis une faute ».

Now a "technical fault"/"a failure": « un défaut » ou « une faille ».

e.g. "There was a technical fault at the factory": « Il y a eu une faille technique à l'usine ».

So, what is the difference between those 3?

Well the standard fault, when you are guilty of something minor is going to be "a fault": « une faute », e.g. "It's my fault we're late".

A serious fault, something that can get you fired or imprisoned, will be « une faute grave ».

"Eric was at fault": « Eric a commis une faute ».

And a technical fault as in "failure" is « un défaut ». [Note: a generic "failure" is « un échec »].

So, we've got all three types and degrees of faults.

Now in the very first one, "it is my fault": « c'est de ma faute », why am I adding « de »?

It's a set phrase. It's just like that. We say « c'est de ma faute » because it is a trace of the Latin genitive case, like we've seen before. It indicates the origin of an event, "the origin of the fault is me": « c'est de ma faute ».

Why am I adding « si » c'est de ma faute, « si » on est en retard »? It is another set phrase with no specific explanation. It's a kind of « si »: "if" that explains the consequence. "It's my fault if we're late".

It's a false conditional because we know we're late, but we're still adding "if we're late" out of politeness.

What's the difference between « on » and « nous »? Why am I using "on est en retard" instead of « nous sommes en retard »? I could actually use either.

« nous » is mostly formal, or personal. I can point my finger at the group of people I'm referring to. « on » is more informal, more impersonal. So wherever you can use « nous », you may use « on » to make it more informal, more impersonal. This doesn't always work the other way around.

- "late": « en retard »

It's an adjective in English, but a nominal group in French. It's a noun with a preposition.

The adjective doesn't exist as such in French, it doesn't mean the same thing. The adjective « retardé » is very different. It means "delayed" or "retarded".

So, "we're late" is « on est en retard »/« nous sommes en retard », as if saying "in delay", "in lateness".

Quick tip: three nuances of faults

Be very careful about the nuances.

« une faute » is not « une erreur ». It's basically the same difference between a fault and an error/a mistake.

« une faute » includes a moral dimension; « une erreur » is just a mistake.

In a legal context, you've got different degrees of seriousness.

For example, a dismissal notice in a company. You've got three levels:

- misdemeanour: faute simple
- misconduct: faute grave
- gross misconduct: faute lourde

24. "a delivery": « une livraison »

Example sentence

"What does our supplier do when he's late on deliveries?"

« Que fait notre fournisseur lorsqu'il est en retard sur les livraisons ?»

Breakdown

- "a supplier": « un fournisseur »
- "TO SUPPLY": « FOURNIR »
- "late": « en retard »
- "on deliveries": « sur les livraisons »

Quick tip: Inversion in a question

Notice that I didn't use « Qu'est-ce que ? » to form my question, but rather an inversion to make it more formal. So instead of saying « Qu'est-ce que notre fournisseur fait ? », I said « Que fait notre fournisseur ? ».

Grammar point: "What"

"what" is usually « ce que » in a statement, not in a question.

In a question, it will be « quel » or « que ».

Let's explain the basics of relative pronouns: "which", "what", "who" and how they are translated. There is no equivalence between English and French. The English makes a distinction between a person and an item. So you will use "which" for an item, "who" for a person, and "what" for both. But in French, it's not a person/item distinction, it's a subject/object distinction. If the person or the item is the subject (is doing the action), you will use a relative pronoun. If it's the object (receiving the action,) you will use another.

For example, « qui » is the subject (active) relative pronoun.

« que » or « ce que » is the object (passive) relative pronoun.

e.g. If I say "Simon is the person who is filming the scene", I will say « Simon est la personne qui filme la scène ». So I'm using "who" in English because Simon is a person, and I'm using « qui » in French, not because Simon is a person, but because Simon is doing the action of filming the scene.

And if I reverse it, "The scene is that which is being filmed by Simon", the French will be « La scène est ce que Simon filme ». I'm using « ce que » because the scene is receiving the action of being filmed by Simon.

25. "a concern": « un sujet de préoccupation »

Example sentence

"The June sales drop is a matter of great concern."

« La baisse des ventes en juin est un sujet important de préoccupation. »

[Note: You can also say *« La baisse des ventes en juin est un sujet de grande préoccupation. »*]

Breakdown

- "a sales drop": « une baisse des ventes »

Remember the English is more practical, and uses vivid images like " drop", whereas the French is more abstract. « la baisse »: "the decrease"

- "June": « juin »

Notice that the English month is upper case, not the French month. Days and titles work the same.

Titles have almost no upper case, except the first noun of novel titles for example. e.g. « L'Ile au trésor » ("Treasure Island", the Robert Louis Stevenson novel).

- "a matter of great concern": « un sujet de grande préoccupation »

Notice that the syntax is similar; "a matter": « un sujet » ; "of": « de » ; "great": « grande », "concern": « préoccupation ».

« CONCERNER » is a false friend. « CONCERNER » is too weak to translate as "CONCERN".

« CONCERNER » is "TO REFER TO"/"TO BE LINKED TO"/"TO RELATE TO".

Quick tip: "A worry"

Something easier to remember for "a concern": « un souci ». That's for a minor worry.

26. "to turn": « transformer »

Example sentence

"He is going to turn the company around in no time."

« *Il va transformer l'entreprise en un rien de temps.* »

Breakdown

- "the company": « l'entreprise »
- "TO TURN something around": « TRANSFORMER quelque chose »

Again, the English uses a very vivid image, "turn around", but the French uses an abstract concept, "TO TRANSFORM": « TRANSFORMER ».

- "in no time": « en un rien de temps ».

The French literally says "in nothing of a time": « en un rien de temps ».

Grammar point: Short term future

"he is going to turn": "il va transformer".

So this is a short term future. It is used to describe future events in the near future, and in a very simple way.

This is the first kind of future that you need to learn, and it works exactly like in English.

In English you would say "I am going to be", and the French is « je vais être ». The only difference is you use "am going", the present perfect in English, which doesn't exist in French.

Therefore, the verb is only one word, « je vais » in present, and then you add the infinitive "TO BE": « ETRE ».

ALLER ETRE – TO BE GOING TO BE
(short term future)

Je vais être	I am going to be
Tu vas être	You are going to be
Il/Elle va être	He/She is going to be
Nous allons être	We are going to be
Vous allez être	You are going to be
Ils/Elles vont être	They are going to be

Let's use another verb, "TO TAKE": « PRENDRE »

ALLER PRENDRE – TO BE GOING TO TAKE
(short term future)

Je vais prendre	I am going to take
Tu vas prendre	You are going to take
Il/Elle va prendre	He/She is going to take
Nous allons prendre	We are going to take
Vous allez prendre	You are going to take
Ils/Elles vont prendre	They are going to take

27. "responsible": « responsable »

Example sentence

"Adults will be responsible for their mistakes."

« Les adultes seront responsables de leurs erreurs. »

Breakdown

- "an adult": « un adulte »

It's transparent, it's the same word, because it comes from Latin.

- "a mistake": « une erreur »
- "responsible for": « responsable de »

Remember, « responsable » is an adjective and as such, you need to match its gender and number with those of the noun.

« Les adultes » is masculine plural, « responsables » need to be masculine plural, so with an extra "s" at the end.

Quick tip: "accountable"

How do you translate that? There is no literal translation. "To be accountable" would be « devoir rendre des comptes ». So literally, "having to give an account of", like in English. It comes from counting or accounting, as in being responsible for the books or the numbers.

Grammar point: Futur simple (simple future)

The « futur simple » is the real, long term future. In English it would be "will be", as in "adults will be responsible": « les adultes seront responsables ».

So we've seen the short term future. Now let's see the real future. It's a longer term future, built like a standard tense. So you've got the regular verbs of the three groups and irregular verbs.

Let's see a regular verb, « PARLER ».

It's a first group verb, so the ending is « -ER ». So future is a bit different, you keep the ending (« -ER » in this case) because the mark of the future is the –r; and after t, you add the endings of the future.

So « PARLER »:

PARLER – TO SPEAK (future)

Je parle-r-ai	I will speak
Tu parle-r-as	You will speak
Il/Elle parle-r-a	He/She will speak
Nous parle-r-ons	We will speak
Vous parle-r-ez	You will speak
Ils/Elles parle-r-ont	They will speak

Now let's see an irregular verb, the one in the example "TO BE": ("will be" in the future).

So let's conjugate « ETRE »:

ETRE – TO BE (future)

Je se-r-ai	I will be
Tu se-r-as	You will be
Il/Elle se-r-a	He/She will be
Nous se-r-ons	We will be
Vous se-r-ez	You will be
Ils/Elles se-r-ont	They will be

28. "a department": « une direction »

Example sentence

"Ten departments but only seven directors, is that best practice?"

« *Dix directions mais seulement 7 directeurs, est-ce que c'est une bonne pratique ?* »

Breakdown

- "a department": « une direction ».
- "but": « mais »
- "only": « seulement »
- "a director": « un directeur » (masculine)/« une directrice » (feminine)
- "is it that": « est-ce que c'est »

Remember how to form a question in French? This is the formal way, "is that": « est-ce que c'est ».

- "best practice": « une bonne pratique »

Quick tip: "best practice"

Why is it like this? It's a well-known management notion, it is very common in English. So it's transparent in French. We just translated it as « bonne pratique ». We don't literally say « la meilleure pratique » ("best practice"), we say "une bonne pratique" (a good practice"). But the notion is still there, you're comparing the practices.

Note: English-savvy executives also use « les best practices ».

Grammar point

In English, "best practice" has no article. « une bonne pratique » has an article. It's just another example where the

French ALWAYS needs an article, but the English chooses not to have one, because it's such a common notion now, a set phrase. But the French always needs an article, « est-ce que c'est une bonne pratique ? » : "is that best practice?".

You need to learn by heart the indefinite article « une », and all other articles:

Definite articles: « le », « la », « les ».

Indefinite articles: « un », « une », « des ».

29. "Lean": « le Lean »

Example sentence

"Our company uses both methodologies to increase productivity, Lean and Six Sigma."

« Notre entreprise utilise les deux méthodologies pour augmenter la productivité, le Lean et le Six Sigma. »

Breakdown

- "a methodology": « une méthodologie »

Transparent because of shared Latin roots.

- "TO INCREASE": « AUGMENTER »
- "a company": « une entreprise »
- "productivity": « la productivité »

Also transparent because of shared Latin roots, but there's no article here in English.

- "TO USE": « UTILISER ».

« USER » also exists but it's not neutral like "to use". « USER » is more "TO ABUSE" or "TO USE too much".

- "both": « les deux »

Literally "the two". There is no such thing as the concept of "both", so we will always say « les deux ».

- "Six Sigma": « Six Sigma »

Another mainstream management term that the French have picked up.

30. "a downsizing": « une réduction d'effectifs »

Example sentence

"The investors were asking HR to begin downsizing."

« *Les investisseurs demandaient aux RH de commencer la réduction d'effectifs.* »

Breakdown

- "the investors": « les investisseurs »
- "were asking": « demandaient »

So, this is « demandaient », "to ask" in the « imparfait ». We'll see how it works in the grammar point.

- "HR": « les RH »

So, HR stands for human resources. Les RH, les ressources humaines. It's just inverted because the English has the noun "human" as the adjective by placing it before. But in French you need the adjective after the noun. So « les ressources humaines », be careful with the S-link. Despite the « h », the link still needs to be made.

Quick tip: "HRD"

To translate acronyms, what you usually do is you simply invert the letters. For example, HRD, the human resources department is going to be « la DRH », « la direction des ressources humaines ». « Le DRH » is the person, the Director of human resources. « La DRH » is either the female Director or the department.

Grammar point: l'imparfait (continuous part)

Uses of l'imparfait: it's a continuous past. Unlike the « passé composé » which is a completed action, a brief event. The imparfait is used to describe ongoing past actions or a past event with a certain duration, a background event or a repeated past event. You use it when you can't use the passé compose, because it's not a brief event.

For instance, "I was running" (« je courais ») is a continuous past (imparfait in French) vs "I ran" (« j'ai couru ») which is a simple past (passé compose in French).

How does it work? You basically need an extra "i" in the middle. For example, let's conjugate « DEMANDER ».

« DEMANDER », first group verb. So, we have the ending "-ER". Remove it and you have the root « demand- ». And you add the endings for « imparfait ».

DEMANDER – TO ASK (imparfait)

Je demand-ais	I asked
Tu demand-ais	You asked
Il/Elle demand-ait	He/She asked
Nous demand-ions	We asked
Vous demand-iez	You asked
Ils/Elles demand-aient	They asked

If you noticed how it's spelled, there is always an "i". The "i" is the mark of « imparfait ».

Quick tip 2: imparfait vs future/conditional

The way to avoiding mixing up « imparfait » with future is to remember this: if there is an "r", it's probably future or conditional. If there is an "i", it's probably « imparfait ». Don't mix them up!

« L'imparfait » is going to be « il demandait », the future is going to be « il demandera ». The conditional would be « il demanderait   ».

31. "cost-cutting": « réduction des coûts »

Example sentence

"The CEO just announced his four-year cost-cutting program."

« *Le PDG vient d'annoncer son plan de réduction des coûts sur quatre ans.* »

Breakdown

- "a program": « un plan »

False Friend alert!

"program" is not « un programme ». « Un programme » is usually used with « programme télé », "a TV program" or a "festival program". « Un plan » is usually what you use for "a program", what you plan to do.

- "just" as in "just announced": « VENIR DE »

We will see this in the grammar point.

- "cost-cutting": « réduction des coûts »

This is an excellent example of a translation that is not literal, because the English uses two nouns with a hyphen in the middle to turn the first one into an adjective, cost and cut: cost-cutting, cutting the cost. The French can't do that. So it has to use two nouns, with « de » or « des » in the middle.

- "The CEO", the Chief Executive Officer is « le Président-Directeur Général », le PDG
- "to announce": « ANNONCER »
- "four-year": « de quatre ans »

The same thing happens as before, the hyphen makes it an adjective, so we have to use « de », the genitive way: « de quatre ans ».

Grammar point: « venir de »

Why did I translate "just" with « venir de »? « Venir de » is a set phrase. Here's how it works. You've got two verbs and the first one will be conjugated, but the second one will stay in the infinitive.

For example, « venir d'annoncer »:

VENIR D'ANNONCER – TO HAVE JUST ANNOUNCED (present)

Je vien-s d'annoncer	I (have) just announced
Tu vien-s d'annoncer	You (have) just announced
Il/Elle vien-t d'annoncer	He/She (has) just announced
Nous ven-ons d'annoncer	We (have) just announced
Vous ven-ez d'annoncer	You (have) just announced
Ils/Elles vienn-ent d'annoncer	They (have) just announced

So we only conjugate « VENIR »; the second verb « ANNONCER » stays in the infinitive. It's a very useful go-to expression in French.

Pay attention to the clue which is « de », it gives away the fact that it's used as a modal verb and not as a common verb. « VENIR » alone is "TO COME". It behaves exactly the same, it's the same verb and you conjugate it the same.

It's like "going to" in English: "going" is a stand-alone verb, which can also be used as a modal verb, thus introducing another verb, e.g. "I'm going to eat".

So you can use « venir de » with any verb: « je viens de manger » ("I just ate"), « je viens de marcher » ("I just walked", « je viens de parler » ("I just talked"), with all 6 persons.

32. "a product": « un produit »

Example sentence

"How many products does each salesman have?"

« De combien de produits chaque commercial dispose-t-il ? »

Breakdown

- "How many?": « Combien ? »

Note that "How much?" is also « Combien ? »

- "a salesman": « un commercial »
- "TO HAVE": « DISPOSER DE ». This is the formal version.

I could have just used « AVOIR »: « Combien de produits chaque commercial a-t-il ? ».

But here you are shown a different register of language.

Quick tip : use formal English

If you want to sound more French, or if you're looking for a good translation, go for formal/very formal English. It often won't be as formal in French, it will be just perfect.

For example, "TO DISPOSE OF", meaning "TO HAVE", is very uncommon and very formal, even posh in English, but it's just a bit formal in French. « De combien de produits chaque commercial dispose t-il »? is not too formal, perfect for a business context.

Be careful about the contraction « DISPOSER DE ». You have to use the preposition « de » before the items that you have, e.g. "the products". And since it's a question, you will place it at the beginning: « De combien ? ».

33. "a mixed picture": « une situation mitigée »

Example sentence

"I wouldn't invest in this company if I were you. Their 2013 financial report is a mixed picture."

« Je n'investirais pas dans cette entreprise si j'étais vous. Leur rapport financier 2013 montre une situation mitigée. »

Breakdown

- "TO INVEST": « INVESTIR »
- "I would invest": « j'investirais »
- "I would not invest": « je n'investirais pas »

This is "TO INVEST": « INVESTIR », in the conditional mode. We will see this mode in the grammar point.

- "If I were you": « si j'étais toi », or « si j'étais vous » (formal)
- "a financial report": « un rapport financier »

Quick tip 1: "reporting"

You only need to say « le reporting » with a very French accent. It's a transparent word because we just borrowed it.

Quick tip 2: "to be a mixed picture": « montrer une situation mitigée »

Why is it so different? It's a set phrase. It's an idiomatic, specific expression in each language. So, what happens is the main verb changes totally. This happens often with idiomatic expressions. Idiomatic expressions are expressions that are specific to a language. The more used they are, the more distorted with time they become. This is why basic verbs in any language, like "TO BE": « ÉTRE »; "TO HAVE": « AVOIR » are so irregular in both languages. With idiomatic expressions and set phrases, you cannot go with literal translations, by definition. You have to be careful with the verb, learn the entire expression by heart; otherwise if you learn just bits and pieces, and it just won't work at all.

As usual, the metaphors will be more practical in English and more abstract in French. Generally speaking, English is a very practical language, and French is a very abstract language. This is partly why the English uses a lot more verbs and nouns, and the French does the opposite, using more nouns than verbs.

For example, "it costs me too much to put up with the situation": « le coût de cette situation est trop important pour moi ». This example is perfect because it's got two things : "it costs me" which is a verb, « le coût » a noun, and it also has a prepositional verb "to put up with", which is made of a very vivid image "to put up with". The translation in French is « trop important », "too important", a more abstract concept.

Grammar point: Conditional

Conditional is a mode, a set of tenses. Why is it used? It expresses an uncertain future event that is bound to a condition. It's used when the English uses "would" or "could" or another modal verb, for uncertain events. So we are using here the conditional present, not the conditional past.

How does it work? [Note: the audio is slightly inaccurate here] You basically take the root from future, and add the endings from imparfait. For example, the future of « INVESTIR » is « investirai » at the first person, its root is « investir- », to which you add the ending of imparfait, « -ais ». Here it is:

INVESTIR – TO INVEST (conditional present)

J'investir-ais	I would invest

Tu investir-ais	You would invest
Il/Elle investir-ait	He/She would invest
Nous investir-ions	We would invest
Vous investir-iez	You would invest
Ils/Elles investir-aient	They would invest

PRENDRE – TO TAKE (conditional present)

Je prendr-ais	I would take
Tu prendr-ais	You would take
Il/Elle prendr-ait	He/She would take
Nous prendr-ions	We would take
Vous prendr-iez	You would take
Ils/Elles prendr-aient	They would take

Do not mix it up with the future. There is an extra "s" compared to the future. This is actually a very common mistake among natives. They will write the verb with an "s" when thinking of future, but the "s" only belongs to the conditional. You know better than them, don't mix them up.

All these modal verbs "WOULD", "COULD", translate into conditional in French, but sometimes you need to add a verb like « pouvoir » or « devoir » in the conditional tense, and the second verb is not conjugated, as usual, it stays in the infinitive. For example:

"I would take": « je prendrais »
"I could take": « je pourrais prendre ».

« pourrais » is « POUVOIR » in the conditional, and then you have « PRENDRE » in the infinitive.

"I should take": « je devrais prendre ».

« devrais » is « DEVOIR » in conditional present, and then you have « PRENDRE » in the infinitive.

34. "successful": « être un succès »

Example sentence

"Look at the sales figures, what a successful product launch."

« Regarde les chiffres des ventes, le lancement du produit a été un vrai succès. »

Breakdown

- "TO LOOK AT": « REGARDER »

It's used here in the imperative mode. We'll see that later, but keep it in mind.

- "the sales figures": « les chiffres des ventes »
- You already know each of these words, but not together "the sales figures": « les chiffres de ventes »
- "a launch": « un lancement »
- "TO LAUNCH" is « LANCER »: « -ER », first group. Easy.
- "a product": « un produit »
- "successful": « être un succès »

The literal translation of successful, as a noun, is impossible. You have to use a paraphrase, another way to say it. So, the alternative is « réussir », for example « le lancement du produit a réussi », or you can use « être un succès », which is what I did.

"a successful product launch": « le lancement du produit a été un succès » is in the passé composé, because it's a past event that is complete.

Quick tip: "What a"

It's an idiomatic, specific English expression of surprise. It doesn't translate literally in French. I used « un vrai succès » to keep the same intensity. It literally means "a real success"/"a true success".

35. "the purpose": « l'objectif »

Example sentence

"What is the main purpose of today's meeting?"

« Quel est l'objectif principal de la réunion d'aujourd'hui ? »

Breakdown

- "main": « principal »

Keep in mind that it's an adjective. So, it needs to be matched in terms of gender and number with the noun « objectif », which is masculine. There are two nouns in the sentence, you might incorrectly think that « réunion » is the main noun.

However, « objectif » is the noun that is linked to the adjective « principal », they go together, so they need to be matched in gender and number. The feminine of « principal » is « principale ».

- "today": « aujourd'hui. "today's": « d'aujourd'hui »

The "'s" is the expression of possession in English, and it is very specific to English. It has to be rendered in French with « de », as usual, the genitive, expressing ownership/origin: « d'aujourd'hui ».

- "What is?: « Quel est ? » or "Which is ?": « Quel est ? »
- "a meeting": « une réunion » or « un meeting »

36. "the vacancies": « les postes vacants »

Example sentence

"We must fill the vacancies. No one is in charge of marketing studies."

« Nous devons pourvoir les postes vacants. Personne n'est responsable des études marketing. »

Breakdown

- "TO FILL the vacancies": « POURVOIR les postes vacants »

It's a set phrase in both languages, so you can't isolate the terms. The verb "TO PROVIDE" is « POURVOIR » ; "TO FILL" (literally) is « REMPLIR », e.g. "TO FILL with water": « REMPLIR avec de l'eau ». So, you are literally providing the seats with someone to fill them.

- "no one": « personne »
- "in charge of": « responsable de »

Be careful: « responsable de » can also translate "responsible for", like we've seen, as in "accountable for".

Someone « responsable de » is either someone "doing the job of"/"occupying a position", or "being accountable for". Closely related, but different.

- "the marketing studies": « les études marketing »

It's mostly transparent, although « études »: "studies" are slightly different. They share the same Latin root, just like « étudiant »: "student".

Quick tip: « POURVOIR » vs « POUVOIR »

Don't confuse « **POURVOIR** » with « **POUVOIR** » ("TO BE ABLE TO"). If you're having trouble, use a synonym like « OCCUPER »: "TO OCCUPY"; « OCCUPER un poste vacant »: "TO FILL a vacancy".

Grammar point: "MUST"

How do you use and translate "MUST" into French? You mainly use the verb « DEVOIR ». Now, "MUST" is grammatically a modal verb. It modifies another verb, and it's not a "real" verb in itself. It's very specific to English, like "SHOULD" and "COULD".

« DEVOIR » behaves like "MUST". It's a standalone verb, but it can also be paired with another verb, like "TO FINISH": « FINIR ».

For example, "I must finish this project": « je dois finir ce projet ».

So, like in English "MUST": « DEVOIR » are the conjugated verbs, and then "TO FINISH" or « FINIR» stay at the infinitive.

Let's conjugate it:

DEVOIR FINIR – TO HAVE TO/MUST FINISH
(present)

Je dois finir	I must finish
Tu dois finir	You must finish
Il/Elle doit finir	He/She must finish
Nous devons finir	We must finish
Vous devez finir	You must finish
Ils/Elles doivent finir	They must finish

37. "to argue": « se disputer »

Example sentence

"My colleagues and I never argue at the office."

« Mes collègues et moi ne nous disputons jamais au bureau. »

Breakdown

- "a colleague": « un collègue »

Transparent. The only exception is, in the south of France, « un collègue » sometimes refers to a friend/buddy.

- "never": « jamais »

Be careful: it's not used the same way with regards to negation. In English you will either say "I never do this" or "I don't ever do this". Double negation is forbidden. In French, you will use « jamais » WITH negation.

e.g. "I never run": « Je ne cours jamais ». In this example, we use « nous ne nous disputons jamais ». « ne » is the first negation and « jamais » is the second negation.

- "the office": « le bureau »
- "at the office": « au bureau »

"at" is usually « à ». « à » + « le » = « au ».

If it were in the feminine, it would be « à » + « la » with no contraction, e.g. "at the beach": « à la plage ».

Quick tip: Contraction of prepositions

Some generic translations of location-related prepositions:

- "At": « au »/« à la »
- "In": « dans »/« en »
- "On": « sur »

Examples:

"at the office": « au bureau »

"at home": « à la maison »

"in the building": « dans le bâtiment »

"on the table": « sur la table »

You also have lots of coastal towns with names like « Villefranche-sur-Mer », « Théoule-sur-Mer », meaning "on the sea"; like many English cities, e.g. "Stratford-upon-Avon". Be very careful with these generic translations. Every good translation is contextual.

Grammar point: Reflexive verbs

We've seen that "my colleagues and I never argue" was translated as « mes collègues et moi ne nous disputons jamais ». I've added the reflexive pronoun « nous », which is not needed in English. It's not necessarily the same verbs in English and French that need the reflexive form/reflexive pronoun. For instance, you have "TO ARGUE": « SE DISPUTER ».

How does it work? The subject of the sentence is doing the action on themselves or on each other, as in "to argue". You conjugate the verb at whatever tense, and you add the reflexive pronoun in the middle. For example, "we argue": « nous nous disputons ».

Let's conjugate « SE DISPUTER », in the present.

SE DISPUTER – TO ARGUE (present)

Je me dispute	I argue
Tu te disputes	You argue
Il/Elle se dispute	He/She argues
Nous nous disputons	We argue

Vous vous disputons	You argue
Ils/Elles se disputant	They argue

Some examples that need this in English: "TO ASK ONESELF": « SE DEMANDER ».

38. "the research": « la recherche »

Example sentence

"Our research suggests that each salesman could promote more products."

« Nos recherches suggèrent que chaque commercial pourrait promouvoir plus de produits. »

Breakdown

- "TO SUGGEST": « SUGGÉRER »
- "that": « que »
- "TO SUGGEST THAT": « SUGGÉRER QUE »
- "a salesman": « un commercial »
- "TO PROMOTE": « PROMOUVOIR »
- "a promotion": « une promotion »
- "more": « plus » or « plus de »

2 different structures. "more" + noun: « plus de »

e.g. "more people": « plus de gens »; "more products": « plus de produits ».

The other structure is "more + adjective".

e.g. "more fun": « plus amusant »; "stronger": « plus fort » (« de » disappears).

Grammar point: "COULD"

"COULD": « pourrait ». "COULD" is another modal verb. You use « POUVOIR » in the conditional present tense.

e.g. "each salesman could promote": « chaque commercial pourrait promouvoir ». If you're struggling with those, here is a quick tip to translate easily: find a synonym like "would be able to": « serait capable de ». It usually works, and it's usually easier to use.

Quick tip: "the research": « les recherches »

Why is it suddenly plural in French? Collective nouns like "research" in English are rare in French, so you need a standard plural in French. You need to add an "s" at the end to make the noun plural; « la recherche » becomes « les recherches ».

Collectives do exist in French but they're rare, e.g. « la foule »: "the crowd"; « la multitude »: "the multitude". When you use them, you may use either the singular or the plural to enhance the collective or individual roles.

e.g. You may use either «une foule de personnes est venue» or « une foule de personnes sont venues ».

39. "an advertisement": « une annonce »

Example sentence

"Can you put out the advertisement for the HR officer position today?"

« Pouvez-vous publier l'annonce pour le poste de responsable RH aujourd'hui ? »

Breakdown

- "CAN" is translated as « POUVOIR »

"CAN" is a modal verb in English, which is very specific. It modifies a verb, and it can only be used with another verb. The French « POUVOIR » can be a standalone verb. But it works just the same.

e.g. "I can do this": « je peux faire ça ». "CAN" is the conjugated verb, "DO" is in the infinitive. Same thing in French, « peux » is conjugated, « FAIRE » is in the infinitive.

- "TO PUT OUT": « PUBLIER »

This is yet another example of a prepositional verb in English. It's a vivid image that is rendered in French with a concept: « PUBLIER »: "TO PUBLISH"/"TO MAKE PUBLIC".

- "HR officer": « responsable RH »

Again, we see that someone who is in charge of something is responsible for it, « responsable RH ».

- "a position": « un poste »

Quick tip: "an advertisement"

When you're advertising for a product or a service, "an advertisement" is « une publicité ». "an ad" (short for advertisement) is « une pub ».

40. "a team": « un service »

Example sentence

"His progression from team manager to director was quick."

« Sa progression de chef de service à directeur a été rapide. »

Breakdown

- "a team" is usually « une équipe » in a general context. But in a business context, « service » is more used.

« équipe » can also be used in a business context when there is a strong anglo influence: "we're all part of a team", « on fait tous partie d'une équipe ».

We also have "team building": « des séminaires de team building ».

- "a team manager" is « un chef de service ». In the manufacturing sector/at a smaller scale, we use « chef d'équipe ». « un chef d'équipe » is usually in charge of a team of workers

- "a director": « un directeur »/« une directrice » (feminine)

For all names of positions and career lexicon, please refer to the relevant extra chapter.

Grammar point: possessive adjectives

"his": « sa ». "his progression": « sa progression »

Those are possessive adjectives [Note: the audio incorrectly says "pronouns"]. They work a little bit differently in English and French. In English, the possessive adjective's gender depends on the **owner's** gender. In French, the possessive adjective's gender depends on the **object's** gender.

e.g. In English you'll use "his wife, "his house", "his male dog", "his female dog". You use "his" because you're talking about the owner and he is male (in this example).

In French, the gender will depend on what you're talking about. For example, "his wife": « sa femme » but "his male dog": « son chien ». And we could be talking about a male owner or female owner, it doesn't matter. What matters is the object's gender. Wife is female, male dog is male, and we change the adjective accordingly.

The 6 possessive adjectives in French are:

POSSESSIVE ADJECTIVES*
(masculine/feminine/plural)

Mon/Ma/Mes	My
Ton/Ta/Tes	Your
Son/Sa/Ses	His/Her
Notre/Notre/Nos	Our
Votre/Votre/Vos	Your
Leur/Leur	Their

*This table is already present in Chapter 21, but with less explanation.

Quick tip: "progress" vs "progression"

Do not mix up "progress" with "progression".

"progress" is « des progrès » (always plural) .

"progression" is « progression » - it's transparent.

e.g. "you've made progress": « tu as fait des progrès ».

But "your progression is good": « ta progression est bonne ».

The difference between "progress": « progrès » and "progression": « progression » = "progress" is incremental steps and "progression" is an overview. So, you need to be careful when you're translating this.

41. "an application": « une candidature »

Example sentence

"Does this company require suppliers to submit an application? No, they have to respond to a call for bids."

« Cette entreprise demande-t-elle aux fournisseurs de déposer une candidature ? Non, ils doivent répondre à un appel d'offre. »

Breakdown

- "TO REQUIRE": « DEMANDER »

False friend alert!

"TO DEMAND" is not « DEMANDER ». "TO DEMAND" is « EXIGER ». There is the same difference in intensity between "TO REQUIRE"/"TO DEMAND" as there is between « DEMANDER » and « EXIGER ». « EXIGER » is much stronger.

Now we've seen how to make a question by inverting, like in English, the subject and the verb: "does this company require?".

The French also inverts: « cette entreprise demande-t-elle » instead of « elle demande ». Like we've seen, this is the formal way of constructing a question.

- "TO SUBMIT": « DÉPOSER »

You may also say « SOUMETTRE », « soumettre une candidature ». "TO SUBMIT" is also usually « SOUMETTRE » in other contexts.

- "a call for bids": « un appel d'offre »

This is the same expression.

"a call", like a phone call, is « un appel »

"a bid" is « une offre ».

- "TO RESPOND": « RÉPONDRE »
- « RÉPONDRE » can also translate "TO ANSWER"

Quick tip: "must"vs "to have to"

We used "TO HAVE TO" as in "MUST". There is a slight difference in English.

"TO HAVE TO" implies an external obligation, e.g. "I have to do my homework": « je dois faire mes devoirs ».

"MUST" usually implies an internal obligation, e.g. "I must change my diet": « je dois changer mon régime ».

See how in French, it's going to be translated as the same word, « DEVOIR », that we've seen before.

Hence "they have to respond" is « ils doivent répondre ».

42. "an interview": « un entretien »

Example sentence

"Let's schedule your job interview on Monday, if you can't, I need to push it to Wednesday."

« Programmons votre entretien d'embauche lundi, si vous ne pouvez pas, je dois le décaler à mercredi. »

Breakdown

- "TO SCHEDULE": « PROGRAMMER », as in "TO PLAN".

Do you remember how "a plan" was usually « un programme »?

- "a schedule": « un emploi du temps » (literally "the use use your time")
- "a job interview": « un entretien d'embauche »

  "an interview" is « un entretien », and « embauche » means hiring. So « un entretien d'embauche » is literally "a hiring interview"
- "Monday": « lundi »

Let's do all seven days:

LES JOURS DE LA SEMAINE – THE DAYS OF THE WEEK

Lundi	Monday
Mardi	Tuesday
Mercredi	Wednesday
Jeudi	Thursday

Vendredi	Friday
Samedi	Saturday
Dimanche	Sunday

- "if you can't ": « si vous ne pouvez pas »

"if" is « si », "you" is « vous », "cannot": « ne pouvez pas »

- "TO PUSH ASIDE": « DÉCALER »
  "to push a meeting to": « décaler une réunion à »

So you "push to Wednesday": « décaler à mercredi ».

Quick tip: Days

You will say on Monday" in English. But we usually say « lundi » and not « à lundi ».

« à lundi » means "see you on Monday".

Dates in French, like in English, use the article « le » except when referring to a day within the next seven-day period.

For example, if I'm talking about this Wednesday and we're Monday, I'm going to say « je le ferai mercredi » instead of « je le ferai le mercredi » ("I will do it on Wednesday"). Also in the past you don't use any article, e.g. « lundi dernier : "last Monday".

However if you're referring to a specific date, e.g. "Monday the 22nd" you will say « le lundi 22 ».

Also days are written in lowercase in French, like months.

Grammar point: The imperative mode

We used "let's" again, "let's schedule: « programmons ». This is imperative, a new mode. Why is it used? It's used to give an order or an instruction.

The way it works is very simple, it only has three different forms instead of 6. For example, « PROGRAMMER » is a first group verb. So let's remove the « -ER » ending, keep the root « programm- » and add the new imperative endings to the three persons used in the imperative: the second one, the fourth one and the fifth one. Let's do it:

PROGRAMMER – TO SCHEDULE/PROGRAM
(imperative present)

Programme	Schedule/Program (You)
Programmons	Let's schedule/program (We)
Programmez	Schedule/Program (Formal or plural You)

Reminder

"Let's" is a soft imperative but there is no such thing in French. So we have to use the strong imperative.

We could have used a strong imperative in English too. Instead of "let's schedule", we could have said "schedule". In both cases, the French is "programmons".

43. "an update": « un point »

Example sentence

"Let's have an update on the marketing file at three pm."

« Faisons un point sur le dossier marketing à 15h (quinze) heures. »

Breakdown

- "let's have" is « faisons ». Imperative.
- "an update": « un point »

"an update" is usually « une mise à jour » but when your boss summons you in their office for an update, the word is then « un point ».

Literally, a "dot (on the map)", it's a metaphor originating from sailing. "to have an update" is « faire un point ».

- "a (physical) file"/"a case": « un dossier »

Be careful: the translation is different in the digital world.

"a digital file" : « un fichier »

"a digital folder": « un dossier »

- "marketing " is obviously « marketing »
- "3 pm": « 15 (quinze) heures »

This is a reminder of how the French clock works.

It's a 24-hour clock. You may also say « three (trois) heures » since there's no possible ambiguity.

Quick tip: "right now"

Here's another way of saying "right now"/"ASAP" in a polite way: "at your earliest convenience" is « dans les plus brefs délais » (literally "in the briefest of delays").

44. "the market share": « la part de marché »

Example sentence

"The sales department is bonused according to its capture of market share."

« La direction des ventes est incentivée sur sa capacité à gagner des parts de marché. »

Breakdown

- "TO BONUS": « INCENTIVER »

"to bonus" is a new management slang term for "to give a bonus according to".

The French imitates the English and uses « incentiver » as in « donner un incentive »/« donner une incitation ».

- "according to": « sur »

It's usually translated as « selon », e.g. "according to my boss, I'm efficient": « selon/d'après mon patron, je suis efficace ».

But in this case, we use « sur » because it implies a cause, how your performance is measured. It's a common set phrase.

- "its capture": « sa capacité à gagner »

In this case you have to paraphrase. You have to keep what we call in French « l'esprit plutôt que la lettre », meaning "the spirit instead of the letter".

It's like in contracts, the spirit of the content is more important than the actual wording.

So, a good translation of "its capture" is a paraphrased translation. A bad translation would be a literal translation. « sa capture » would not mean anything.

Another good example: "The sales department captures the market share."

« La direction de ventes gagne/a la capacité de gagner des parts de marché. »

Quick tip: Articles and how to be fluent in French

We've seen that French has more articles.

"market share" becomes « les parts de marché ».

I use the definite article « les » and I use it in the plural because « parts de marché » is collective here [Note: The audio says "uncountable"], it's usually used in the plural.

Don't be afraid to use many articles. Every noun needs an article before it. Better be safe than sorry. If you're having trouble with your articles and prepositions, for example you can't remember how to say « sur » or « de », and if you can't remember the genders, try to break down the longer sentences into two or three shorter ones.

For example, you could say "All departments are measured according to performance. In the sales department, it's measured with market share."

So that would be: « Toutes les directions sont évaluées sur leurs performances. En vente, la performance est évaluée avec la part de marché. »

Don't get stuck with long sentences. Start slow: when you're thinking in English, you're thinking about advanced complex sentences with multiple clauses. Stop doing that in French. Start simple with basic sentences, the listener will be more patient because you're ending your sentences one after the other, you will be less paralyzed and more fluent.

45. "the supply chain": « la supply chain »

Example sentence

"The supply chain department is probably the one where having detailed processes is the most important."

« La direction supply chain est probablement celle où il est le plus important d'avoir des processus détaillés. »

Breakdown

- "probably": « probablement »

They're both adverbs. In English, forming adverbs is really easy, you usually remove the final letter or letters and add "-ly", e.g. gently, unfortunately. In French, you use the matching adjective, put it in the feminine form and then you add « -ment » at the end.

e.g. « doux » ("gentle")/feminine « douce » ("gentle")/adverb « doucement » ("gently").

« malheureux » ("unfortunate")/feminine « malheureuse » ("unfortunate")/adverb « malheureusement » ("unfortunately").

- "where": « où »
- "detailed": « détaillés »

It's an adjective, so be careful with the gender and number.

Here we have « processus », masculine plural.

Hence « détaillés », masculine plural, with « -es » at the end.

Quick tip: Order of the last clause

"Having detailed processes is the most important":

The key words are "having detailed processes". In English you can say "having detailed processes", thus starting the sentence with "having", which is a gerund (verbal form).

In French you can't do that. You could say « le fait d'avoir des processus détaillés » : "the fact of having detailed processes", but you will usually just say « le plus important est d'avoir des processus détaillés ». So you slightly change the order.

Quick tip: "the supply chain"

Why am I using « la supply chain » ? I could use « la chaîne d'approvisionnement », which is the rightful standard French translation. But in most multinationals/big corporations, these terms will be borrowed from the English. This is very common.

However, be careful, in some environments you will be required to use the French terms. For example, in the manufacturing sector, or if your audience doesn't speak English at all.

Grammar point: comparatives and superlatives

We've seen "the most important" in the sentence.

Like in English, a comparative adds "more" or "less" to an adjective.

"more" is « plus », "less" is « moins ».

e.g "more fun": « plus d'amusement ».

In English, there are exceptions and irregular comparatives.

e.g. "stronger"

In French, there are no exceptions. "stronger" will be « plus fort » ; "calmer" will be « plus calme » ; "less difficult" will be « moins difficile ».

The superlative is really similar to the English too.

"the most": « le plus »/« la plus »/« les plus », depending on the gender and number of the adjective.

You're using these when you're comparing something to something else, and one is greater/greatest or worse/ worst. In French, like in English, you have regular and irregular ones.

The regular ones will be constructed with "more": « plus » ; "less": « moins », "the most": « le plus ».

The irregular ones will be like in English : "better": "best". So "better" is « meilleur » ; "best" is « le meilleur ». "Worse" is « pire » ; "the worst" is « le pire ».

However, French has much fewer irregular ones. It's usually the most common words that are the most distorted words.

46. "a rise": « une augmentation »

Example sentence

"We've known a steady rise in market share for two years, let's hope it continues."

« Nous avons connu une hausse régulière de notre part de marché depuis deux ans, espérons que ça continue. »

Breakdown

- "TO KNOW" is either « CONNAÎTRE » or « SAVOIR »

In English, "to know" can be broken down into three different meanings:

- "to know someone" is « connaître quelqu'un »
- "to know a fact" is « SAVOIR un fait »/« SAVOIR quelque chose »
- "TO KNOW" as in "TO EXPERIENCE" is also « CONNAÎTRE », e.g. « nous avons connu /« nous avons fait l'expérience »: "we have experienced a steady rise"
- "steady": « régulier » as in "constant"

e.g. "a constant evolution": « une évolution régulière »/« une hausse régulière »

- "for two years": « depuis deux ans »
- "let's hope": « espérons »

As we've seen, "let's" is the soft imperative and needs to be translated as the hard imperative in French.

The infinitive of the verb is « ESPERER ».

- "let's hope": « espérons »
- "let's hope that": « espérons que »

Remember, in English you may skip "that", but you can't do it in French. "let's hope it continues": « espérons **que** ça continue »

- "it" (third person neutral) doesn't exist in French, so you need to use « ça » or « cela ».

« cela » is the formal version, « ça » is the shorter, informal version.

- "TO CONTINUE": « CONTINUER ». "it continues": « ça continue »/« cela continue »

Quick tip: "since" vs "for"

What's the difference?

"since" is a set date in time and it will be rendered as « depuis ».

e.g. "since 1998": « depuis 1998 »

"for" implies a duration.

e.g. "We've been doing this for over two years": « ça fait deux ans que nous faisons cela ».

Don't mix it up with "ten years ago": « il y a dix ans ».

47. "to achieve": « atteindre »

Example sentence

"Our short term goals need to be achieved before envisioning any long term solution."

« Nos objectifs à court terme doivent être atteints avant d'envisager une solution à long terme. »

Quick tip: Quasi-homonyms

Don't mix up « ATTEINDRE » ("to achieve") with « ATTENDRE » ("to wait").

Breakdown

- "a goal": « un objectif »
- "a long term solution": « une solution à long terme »

We could have removed the preposition « à »: "une solution long terme". Same with "short term": « court terme ».

- "before (doing something)": « avant (de faire quelque chose) »

In English the syntax is "before" + verb in -ing form, e.g. "before envisioning". In French you say « avant de » + verb in the infinitive, e.g. « avant d'envisager ».

- "TO ENVISION": « ENVISAGER ».

You can also say "to consider" in English. But "to envision" is a bit more formal than « ENVISAGER » in French.

- "TO CONSIDER": « ENVISAGER »

False friend alert!

« CONSIDÉRER » is not "TO CONSIDER".

« CONSIDÉRER » has less intensity, it's neutral, it's like "TO THINK" e.g. "I think this is good": « je considère que c'est bon ».

- "a solution" is just « une solution ».

Quick tip: Buying time in conversation, as you prepare your thoughts

When you are having a conversation and you're struggling or you need to buy time, just list the different steps or different points you're about to make.

For example, you will say "the first step is": « la première étape est de » or "the first thing: « la première chose » or "the first level": « premier niveau » and so on.

This will help you buy time and your listeners will be more patient, you will catch their attention.

Go slow, remember, build small sentences.

48. "the performance": « la performance »

Example sentence

"All employees are measured annually on their performance."

« Tous les employés sont évalués annuellement sur leurs performances. »

Breakdown

- "an employee": « un employé »

You can also say « un salarié ». This refers to "the wage" which is « un salaire ».

- "TO MEASURE ": « MESURER »

You can also say « ÉVALUER ». The difference is: « MESURER » is more practical. You measure something on a scale, whereas « ÉVALUER »: "to evaluate" is a bit more abstract.

- "annually": « annuellement »

Remember, this is how you make an adverb. In English, you need to have "-ly" at the end, e.g. "annually".

In French you take the feminine adjective « annuelle » and you add the « -ment » suffix at the end : « annuellement ».

Quick tip: Periodical adjectives

"monthly": « mensuelle »

"weekly": « hebdomadaire »

"daily": « quotidien »

In English, those can both be adverbs and adjectives, depending on the context. In French, they're just adjectives.

e.g. « une réunion mensuelle »/« hebdomadaire »/« quotidienne ».

Another common example: "on the due date": « à l'échéance ».

And a common slang term: « un weekly » is a weekly department meeting.

49. "a campaign": « une campagne »

Example sentence

"The advertising campaign was very successful this year."

« La campagne de publicité a été un franc succès cette année. »

Breakdown

- "advertising": « la publicité »
- "promotion": « promotion »
- "an ad" (advertisement): « une pub »
- "to be successful": « avoir du succès »

Remember this one: we had to use a paraphrase because the noun « succès » has to be used here.

There is no adjective like "successful" in French. You could use an adjective like « prospère »: "prosperous" but the meaning would be slightly different.

This is for your next level language learning. Literal translations often won't work with complex ideas. So the next level for you would be to think in the target language, in French, directly. Right now you're most often thinking of ideas in English and then translating them.

There are many different expressions that are built differently in English and in French.

For example, "I am fifteen": « j'ai quinze ans » (literally "I have fifteen years").

The English uses the verb "to be". In French we use the verb "TO HAVE": « AVOIR ».

The same goes with "to be cold": « avoir froid » ; "to be hungry": « avoir faim ».

- "very": « très ». This is a generic translation that works in most cases
- "very successful": « un franc succès »

So what I did here is that I used the set phrase in French « avoir du succès », and in order to translate the intensity of "very", I had to use the adjective « franc » (literally "frank") : "this was a frank success"/"a real success"/"a true success". This conveys the same idea as "very successful".

e.g. « La campagne a été un franc succès ».

Quick tip: Use synonyms to fight paralysis

If you get blocked, paralyzed trying to find a translation, look for a formal, or slightly different synonym. Even if their meaning is slightly different, it's better than going blank for fifteen seconds.

For example, if you can't think of a translation for "successful" because « avoir du succès » is different, think of "prosperous": « prospère » (transparent).

And if you can't remember « prospère », you can say it in English: "Pardon, en anglais/in English I would say 'prosperous'".

Most people will understand.

Grammar point: Preterit/Present perfect=Passé composé

We used the passé composé in French, « a été ». However, the English was not "has been" (present perfect).

The English used "was" (preterit): "the campaign was successful".

The English has to use preterit (past tense) because there's a date ("this year").

But the French only has one tense to use for a brief event in the past, and that is passé composé (there's a formal, literary equivalent, le passé simple, which is only ever used in literature nowadays).

Here's a quick reminder on how to conjugate it. Let's conjugate « ETRE » in the passé composé:

ETRE – TO BE (passé composé)

J'ai été	I have been/was
Tu as été	You have been/were
Il/Elle a été	He/She has been/was
Nous avons été	We have been/were
Vous avez été	You have been/were
Ils/Elles ont été	They have been/were

So you conjugate the auxiliary which is « AVOIR »: "TO HAVE", then you put « ETRE » in the past participle (its gender or number doesn't change): « il a été », « nous avons été » and so on ; « été » doesn't change.

50. "the capital": « le capital »

Example sentence

"In order to raise capital, a startup needs to be convincing."

« Afin de lever du capital, une start-up a besoin d'être convaincante. »

Breakdown

- "in order to": « afin de »

This is a logical connective, a word that is used to link two sentences or two clauses together.

It's very useful to structure your speech or your emails. Please refer to the standard chapter on logical connectives to know more.

- "a startup": « une start-up »

This is again a borrowed word but you need to be careful with the French pronunciation. The English language is usually conservative with borrowed words, you don't really change them, but the French does, especially the pronunciation.

So let's hear the difference again: "a startup": « une start-up ».

The "r" is very guttural, it starts from your throat. And the last syllable is stressed.

- "NEED": « AVOIR BESOIN DE »

"NEED" is a semi-modal verb, it behaves like a modal verb, just like "MUST" or "CAN".

So here we use « AVOIR BESOIN DE ». We paraphrase because we don't have such a verb. We could have used « DEVOIR » ("MUST") if it were "HAVE TO". The meanings are very similar.

We could have said "a startup must be convincing" and it would be « une start-up doit être convaincante ».

- "convincing": « convaincant »

This is an adjective. So the feminine would be « convaincante », and the feminine plural would be « convaincantes ».

Grammar point: The gender of adjectives

Remember all adjectives need to have the same gender and number as their corresponding noun. Usually to feminise an adjective you only need to add a final « -e ». This is only a rule of thumb and there are lots of exceptions.

So for example, « convaincant » is singular masculine. The plural masculine would be « convaincants » with an « -s ». Singular feminine is « convaincante », final « -e ». Feminine plural is « convaincantes », final « -es ».

51. "customer data": « les données clients »

Example sentence

"You're still using Excel to manage your customer data?"

« Tu utilises encore Excel pour gérer tes données clients ? »

Breakdown

- "you are using": « tu utilises »

Remember there are two presents in English, the standard present "you use" and the present continuous "you are using" [the audio mistakenly says « present perfect »]. There is only one present in French so even if you have to say "you're still using", you will be saying « tu utilises ».

If you really want to enhance the fact that it's an ongoing action, you'll be using « tu es en train d'utiliser » - which is not the case here.

- "still": « encore »
- "Excel": « Excel »

Please note that there is an extra chapter for you to refer to, which broaches software vocabulary like Excel.

- "TO MANAGE": « GÉRER »

« MANAGER », the French-English word, also exists but it doesn't apply to objects.

So you can't use it for "to manage your customer data", you have to use « gérer des données clients ».

- "data": « les données »
- "your customer data": « tes données clients »

Quick tip: « tes données clients »

Notice how we didn't use « des » as in « les données des clients » (we could have).

That's because « les données clients » is a set phrase, a very common phrase in business French.

So if you want to sound street smart or corporate smart remember this.

This happens elsewhere with other common expressions.

Quick tip: How to make an informal question

Do you remember how to make an informal question?

You just need to add a question mark at the end and use an rising inflection.

52. "a database": « une base de données »

Example sentence

"You need a real database to automate your tickets."

« *Tu as besoin d'une vraie base de données pour automatiser tes tickets.* »

Breakdown

- "a database": « une base de données »

This is typical of how different syntax is in English and French. Again, in English you have two nouns and you just juxtapose them and it makes a new compound noun.

The first one becomes a de facto adjective "data", "a base of data" ("database").

But French doesn't do that, « une base de données »: you use one noun + « de » + another noun.

Also, you will need to make « données » plural because you obviously have lots of data.

So you will never be able to write « une base de données » without the -s at the end.

- "you need (something)": « tu as besoin (de quelque chose) »

Many verbs are built differently. The English "you need" doesn't have a preposition after it, the French does: « tu as besoin **de** ».

- "TO AUTOMATE": « AUTOMATISER »

[Note: the audio is inaccurate for this paragraph]

This a rare trap. It should be « AUTOMATER ». The "-is" syllable is added.

In this case, both languages usually have the same number of syllables, e.g. "TO FACILITATE": « FACILITER », "TO ESTIMATE": « ESTIMER ».

- "a ticket": « un ticket » (in the context of customer service)

53. "the earnings": « les revenus »

Example sentence

"Sales are up this quarter but earnings are stable because production costs have risen."

« Les ventes ont augmenté ce trimestre mais les revenus sont stables, car les coûts de production ont grimpé. »

Breakdown

- "the earnings": « les revenus »

In English, "earnings" comes from "to earn".

- "revenue": « le revenu ». The French comes from « REVENIR »: "TO COME BACK".

So, your revenue, your earnings are the portion of your investment that comes back, it's your return on investment. By the way, the acronym "ROI" is also used in French for « retour sur investissement ».

- "sales": « les ventes »
- "TO BE UP" ("TO INCREASE"): « AUGMENTER »

This is yet another example of the English being more straightforward, action-driven: "to be up"; whereas the French is more conceptual.

- "this quarter": « ce trimestre »
- "stable": « stable »

Again, don't forget to match the gender and number of the noun.

- « les revenus sont stables », masculine plural, so « stables » needs to have an « -s »
- "the production costs": « les coûts de production ».

Again, two nouns in English, "production costs", and in French « coûts **de** productions »: "costs **of** production".

- "TO RISE": « GRIMPER »

In this case, both are practical images. « GRIMPER » means "TO CLIMB" as in to climb a ladder, a mountain. « GRIMPER » is the infinitive, and we used the past participle.

For a first-group verb like « GRIMPER », conjugation is very easy. You remove the « -ER » ending, so you've got the root « grimp- », and you add an « -e » with an upwards accent (un accent aigu): « grimpé ».

So « Les coûts de production ont grimpé »: "The production cost have risen".

54. "a deposit": « un dépôt »

Example sentence

"All the deposits on made on this bank account."

« Tous les dépôts sont faits sur ce compte en banque. »

Breakdown

- "all": « tout » or « tous »

"all" is universal whereas « tous » is an adjective, and as such, it needs to be matched in gender and number with the related noun.

Its different forms are: « tout » (masculine singular), « tous » (masculine plural), « toute » (feminine singular) and « toutes » (feminine plural).

- "made": « faits »

This is the passive voice of "TO MAKE" ("made"): « FAIRE » (« faits »).

Usually "TO MAKE" is « FABRIQUER » but in some expressions, "TO MAKE" is going to be « FAIRE ».

Grammar point: The passive voice

In the passive voice, the subject is receiving the action, as opposed to doing it (like in a normal statement). It's used to emphasize the action over the actor.

For example, "the project was terminated" instead of "I terminated the project".

"the project was terminated" is « le projet a été annulé ».

By whom? We don't know.

The passive voice is slightly more common in English and is also used when you want to translate the French « on », the impersonal third person.

e.g. « on a annulé le projet ». « on » doesn't point at anybody. "the project was terminated."

The way to use the passive voice in English and in French is the same.

You first use a verbal form in whatever tense, and then the main verb as a past participle.

Instead of saying "we terminated the project" you say "the project was terminated".

« on a annulé le projet » becomes « le projet a été annulé ».

- "this" is « ce » (masculine singular) or its different forms: « cette » (feminine singular), « cettes » (feminine plural), « ces » (masculine plural). It's a demonstrative article, an article that demonstrates, shows something. Since it's an article, it needs to matched in gender and number
- "on": sur"

For more words related to banking, please refer to the specific chapter at the end of this book.

55. "an engagement": « un rendez-vous »

Example sentence

"I have a previous business engagement on that time slot. I'm sorry."

« *J'ai déjà un rendez-vous professionnel sur ce créneau horaire. Je suis désolé.* »

Breakdown

- "an engagement": « un rendez-vous »

You also have "engaged" as for a phone: « occupé ».

e.g. "The phone was engaged so I hung up.": « Le téléphone était occupé donc j'ai raccroché. »

- "previous": « précédent »/« précédente » (feminine).

Here I paraphrased it as "I already have a business engagement »: « j'ai déjà un rendez-vous ».

"I have a previous engagement" or "I have a prior engagement" or "previous business engagement" is an idiomatic, specific English phrase, so I can't translate it literally. The English uses an adjective, "previous" or "prior", where the French uses the adverb « déjà »: "yet".

- "a time slot": « un créneau horaire »
- "I'm sorry": « je suis désolé »

You need to match this in terms of gender and number because « désolé » is an adjective.

A woman would say « je suis désolée ».

In short it would be "sorry": « désolé ».

Quick tip: Rendez-vous or date?

"rendez-vous" as in a date is « un rendez-vous » or sometimes in slang « un rencard ».

"a (professional) engagement" is also « un rendez-vous ».

So basically, everything in French is « un rendez-vous » except the slang for a date « un rencard ».

56. "to fill out": « REMPLIR »

Example sentence

"Applying to this job requires you to fill out a very complex form."

« Pour candidater à ce poste, il faut remplir un formulaire très complexe. »

Breakdown

- "TO APPLY TO": « POSTULER A » or « CANDIDATER A »
- « CANDIDATER » is a trendy new word based on « candidat »: "a candidate".

But it is less elegant because it artificially turns a noun into a verb, which is a very English thing to do, but not French. However, « postuler » would be redundant with « poste » and with « pour » in terms of pronunciation, so that's why I used « candidater ».

- "applying": « pour candidater ».

This is very common in English, because the English loves verbs.

This -ing form doesn't exist in French. We have to use a noun or, like here, a preposition + a verb, « pour candidater ».

- "TO FILL OUT": « REMPLIR »

"to fill out a form": « remplir un formulaire »

"to fill in a form": « remplir un formulaire »

Even "TO FILL UP" something is « REMPLIR »: there is only one word in French for "fill".

- "very": « très »

- "complex": « complexe »

Quick tip: « très » versus « trop »

« très »: "very"; « trop »: "too much"/"too many".

But in youth slang, you usually use « trop bien », even if you only mean « très bien ».

« trop bien »/« trop cool » means "so good"/"so cool". They tend to exaggerate.

It's like "ever" or "literally". By the way, "literally" means in French « littéralement », it's also used in youth slang, e.g. « c'est littéralement trop cool ».

57. "innovation": « l'innovation »

Example sentence

"Our company succeeds through innovation not imitation."

« *Notre entreprise réussit grâce à l'innovation et non l'imitation.* »

Breakdown

- "a company": « une entreprise »

"our company": « notre entreprise »

- "TO SUCCEED": « RÉUSSIR »

Remember we had "to be successful": « avoir du succès ».

In this case, it's a very simple translation - "TO SUCCEED": « RÉUSSIR », also a verb.

- "through": in this case « grâce à ».

"through" is literally « à travers », and « grâce à » is literally "thanks to".

Here, we have a set phrase: "through innovation": « grâce à l'innovation ».

"not": « et non » in this case. I added the « et » to make it more oral, more fluid.

"imitation", like "innovation", is transparent in French.

- "imitation": « l'imitation »
- "innovation": « l'innovation »

That's because they all come from Latin.

Do you remember the « -tion » rule?

Any noun with « -tion » sounds like "-sion" in English, and is going to be transparent.

58. "internal": « interne »

Example sentence

"That's an internal issue, don't wash your dirty laundry in public."

« *C'est un problème interne, ne lavez pas votre linge sale en public.* »

Breakdown

- "an issue": « un problème »

False friend alert!

« une issue » is "an exit", not "an issue".

- "don't wash" is an imperative in the negative form.

So the negative form in French is usually « ne » + word + « pas »: « ne pas ». Then you put the main word, the verb here, in the middle, "don't wash"; « ne lavez pas ».

- "your": « votre » (formal) or « ton » (informal)
- "your dirty laundry": « votre linge sale ».

The "dirty laundry" expression is exactly the same in French: "don't wash your dirty laundry in public": « ne lavez pas votre linge sale en public ».

- "in": « en »
- "in public": « en public »
- "the public": « le public »

59. "managerial": « managérial »

Example sentence

"You need to make a managerial decision, it's your job."

« Tu dois prendre une décision managériale, c'est ton rôle. »

Breakdown

- "TO NEED TO": « DEVOIR »

In this case we're not going to use « avoir besoin de » because it's an external obligation, so we use « devoir ».

- "to make a decision": « prendre une decision ».

Be careful here. "TO MAKE" should be « FAIRE ».

But in this case, it's a set phrase and we always say « prendre une décision ».

Many times, with set phrases, the main verb is going to change according to the specific image that the language uses.

- "it's your job": « c'est ton rôle » or « c'est ton travail ».

"job" literally means « travail », but in this case it's more accurate to describe someone's role, someone's duty.

Let's break them down, these three notions, three shades of moral obligation: "job", "role" and "duty".

- "a job" is « un travail »
- "a role" is « un rôle »
- "a duty" is « un devoir ».

60. "the opening hours": « les horaires d'ouvertures ».

Example sentence

"Make sure to put the opening hours on the website."

« N'oublie pas de mettre les horaires d'ouverture sur le site web. »

Breakdown

- "TO MAKE SURE" is literally « S'ASSURER QUE ». "make sure" (imperative): « n'oublie pas ». You may use the formal « vous » (formal "you") in the imperative, it will be « n'oubliez pas ». « oublier » means: "to forget". « n'oublie pas »: "don't forget"

But here's a translation tip for you: « ne pas oublier », conjugated, is much more common.

"don't forget to": « n'oublie pas de »

- "TO PUT" or "TO PLACE": « METTRE »

This is a very generic translation. Be careful, for a prepositional verb like "to put off" or "to put on", you're not going to use « mettre » in French, e.g "TO PUT OFF" is « RETARDER ». "TO PUT ON": « ENFILER/PLACER ». Adding a preposition to a verb in English often changes its meaning completely.

- "the website": « le site web »/« le site internet »

61. "to pick up someone": « aller chercher quelqu'un »

Example sentence

"I'll pick you up from the airport after the meeting."

« *J'irai te chercher à l'aéroport après la réunion.* »

Breakdown

- "the airport": « l'aéroport »
- "from": usually « de »/« depuis », indicating the origin.

Here we will use the equivalent of "at the airport": « à l'aéroport ».

- "after": « après »
- "the meeting": « la réunion »/« le meeting »
- "I will pick you up": « j'irai te chercher »

Future Tense Conjugations

Let's try a first group verb first, « PARLER »:

PARLER – TO SPEAK (future)

Je parlerai	I will speak
Tu parleras	You will speak
Il/Elle parlera	He/She will speak
Nous parlerons	We will speak
Vous parlerez	You will speak
Ils/Elles parleront	They will speak

Now let's conjugate the verb that we're using here in the sentence, « aller ».

ALLER – TO GO (future)

J'irai	I will go
Tu iras	You will go
Il/Elle ira	He/She will go
Nous irons	We will go
Vous irez	You will go
Ils/Elles iront	They will go

As you can see, it's highly irregular.

What we're saying in French is literally "I will go to fetch you at the airport": « j'irai te chercher à l'aéroport ».

62. "a quote": « un devis »

Example sentence

"Could you quote me a price to print a hundred business cards?"

« Peux-tu me donner un devis pour l'impression de cent cartes de visites ?»

Breakdown

- "a quote": « un devis »
- "TO QUOTE" is « DONNER UN DEVIS »
- "a price": « un prix »

But "price" is implicit in French here.

You can never say « un devis de prix » like you do in English, e.g. "quote me a price".

- "TO PRINT": « IMPRIMER »

In this case the noun is preferable: "the printing": « l'impression ». We could say « pour imprimer ».

- "a price to print": « un devis pour imprimer »

As usual, French likes nouns better: « un devis pour l'impression ».

- "a business card": « une carte de visite » (literally "a visiting card").

At the time of brick and mortar businesses, you needed the address to visit back, hence, « une carte de visite ».

63. "a brick and mortar shop": « un point de vente »

Example sentence

"This e-commerce company's newest strategy is to set up brick and mortar warehouses."

« La nouvelle stratégie de cette entreprise d'e-commerce est de construire des entrepôts physiques. »

Breakdown

- "a brick and mortar shop": « un point de vente » or « un magasin physique ».

    "a warehouse": « un entrepôt »

    "brick and mortar warehouses": « des entrepôts physiques »

- "a company": « une entreprise »
- "e-commerce": « l'e-commerce »

That's a borrowed word again.

- "a strategy" « une stratégie »
- "newest": « le nouveau »

Technically a superlative, "the newest"="the most recent": « le plus récent »/« la plus récente » (feminine).

But here, the simple adjective « nouvelle » (feminine of « nouveau ») is enough.

We could say « la stratégie la plus récente »: "the most recent strategy".

- "TO SET UP": « CONSTRUIRE » or « ÉTABLIR ».

« CONSTRUIRE » is the physical meaning, e.g. "to build something."

« ÉTABLIR » is, like "establish", more abstract, e.g. « ÉTABLIR sa domination » : "to establish your domination".

- "a warehouse": « un entrepôt ».

64. "to run out": « ne plus avoir de »

Example sentence

"We've run out of paper for the printer, do you know where the spare is kept?"

« On n'a plus de pour l'imprimante, sais-tu où se trouvent les réserves ? »

Breakdown

- "we": « on »

Remember this is the informal "we". The formal "we" is « nous ».

Since this is a very informal situation in the office, I chose the informal « on ».

- "paper": « le papier »

Like in English, you can say "papers" when you mean documents, « des papiers ».

e.g. « Vos papiers, s'il vous plaît » : "Your documents, please".

- "a printer": « une imprimante »
- "TO KNOW": « SAVOIR »

Let's conjugate it. It's a third group verb, pretty irregular.

SAVOIR – TO KNOW (present)

Je sais	I know
Tu sais	You know
Il/Elle sait	He/She knows
Nous savons	We know
Vous savez	You know

| Ils/Elles savont | They know |

- "the spare": « les réserves »

Literally "the reserves", as in "the stocks".

- "kept": « se trouvent »

So in English, the passive voice is used here, "the spare is kept".

That is rendered in French with a pronominal verb, « se trouver ».

- « les réserves se trouvent » as in "the spares can be found" or "are found".

Since it's a question, we inverted the subject and the verb. Instead of « tu sais », we have « sais-tu ».

65. "to state": « formuler »

Example sentence

"Kindly state your request and the customer service will handle it."

« Veuillez formuler votre requête et le service client s'en chargera. »

Breakdown

- "kindly": « veuillez »

"kindly" would literally be « gentiment » in French.

But the French tweaks it into « veuillez », which means "please wish to".

« veuillez » is the imperative tense of « VOULOIR » ("TO WANT"). It's a very soft order, as in "please wish to state your request": « veuillez formuler votre requête ».

- "a request": « une requête »

  "a query" in IT is also une « requête »

- "TO HANDLE": « S'OCCUPER DE »/« SE CHARGER DE ».

So you see that the syntax is different. The English "TO HANDLE" is transitive direct, meaning it doesn't need a preposition between the verb and the object: "TO HANDLE SOMETHING".

But the French « S'OCCUPER DE » or « SE CHARGER DE » are both transitive indirect, so they need the preposition « de » between the verb and the object.

Quick tip: Using « en » to avoid repeating yourself

The original sentence is « le service client s'**en** chargera ». It's akin to saying « le service client se chargera **de** votre requête ».

« en » refers to the first noun that we used in the sentence, « votre requête ». « en » is like "it": it avoids repeating the noun that you've used before.

Here's another example.

"I'm in charge of **this project**" > "I'm in charge of **it**"

Is in French:

« Je suis responsable **de ce projet** » > « J'**en** suis responsable »

66. "to carry out": « mener à bien »

Example sentence

"We've just carried out a survey on customer satisfaction."

« Nous venons de mener (à bien) une enquête sur la satisfaction client. »

Breakdown

- "TO CARRY OUT": « MENER A BIEN » or simply « MENER ».

as in « Nous venons de mener une enquête ».

- "JUST": « VENIR DE »

Do you remember how this works? « VENIR **de** » conjugates like « VENIR » but you add « de », and it now means you've just done something, e.g. "we've **just** carried out": « nous venons de mener ».

- "a survey" is « une enquête ».

Don't mix it up with "a poll": « un sondage ».

"TO POLL": « SONDER »

- "on": « sur »

That's a very generic translation.

We could also have used « de la », e.g. « une enquête de la satisfaction client », which is a good translation for "a survey into customer satisfaction".

- "customer satisfaction" means « la satisfaction client ».

There is no article in English because it's a marketing concept now. And notice that there is no « de » in French either. It's a short, informal way of saying « la satisfaction des clients » or « la satisfaction du client ».

It's specialized jargon now, it's very common. See also: "customer data base": « la base de données client ».

67. "a workshop": « un atelier »

Example sentence

"Workshops are extremely efficient to get group tasks done."

« Les ateliers sont extrêmement efficaces pour mener à bien les tâches collectives. »

Breakdown

- "workshops": « les ateliers »
- "extremely": « extrêmement »

Remember, "-ly" is the usual ending of an adverb in English. In French it will be « -ment » or « -ement ».

- "efficient": « efficace »

Theoretically there is a difference between "efficient" and "effective".

"efficient" is when you use minimal resources to reach your goal.

"effective" is something that allows you to reach the objective really well.

So "efficient" is « efficient » (transparent). And "effective" is « efficace ».

But in both languages, we abuse these meanings and we only use "efficient" and « efficace ».

We don't really mean minimal resources, we usually mean we've reached our goals - "efficient": « efficace ».

- "TO GET SOMETHING DONE": « POUR MENER QUELQUE CHOSE A BIEN ».

"**to** get group tasks done": this "to" indicates an objective.

The generic translation is « pour », e.g. « pour mener à bien ».

And "to get something done" is « mener quelque chose à bien ».

- "a group task": « une tâche collective ».

Again, English likes to use another noun as an adjective: "group task"="a task in group."

French uses another construction: noun + adjective.

Or sometimes: noun + « de »/« des » + other noun.

Remember in French, most adjectives are placed after the noun - "a group task": « une tâche collective ».

Don't forget the gender and number agreement: « une tâche » is singular feminine, so « collectif » becomes « collective » (singular feminine too).

68. "a wage": « un salaire »

Example sentence

"The variable component of wages often depends on skill."

« La part variable des salaires dépend souvent de la compétence. »

Breakdown

- "the variable component": « la part variable ». Literally "the variable part"
- "often": « souvent »
- "TO DEPEND ON": « DEPENDRE DE ».

Be careful with the preposition here. You might expect « dépendre **sur** » but it's actually « **de** ».

This is a very common mistake with my clients when they speak French and try English or the other way around, they will often get the prepositions wrong.

Let's conjugate « DEPENDRE DE »:

DEPENDRE – TO DEPEND ON (present)

Je dépends de	I depend on
Tu dépends de	You depend on
Il/Elle dépend de	He/She depends on
Nous dépendons de	We depend on
Vous dépendez de	You depend on
Ils/Elles dépendent de	They depend on

This is a third group regular verb. Very useful as a reference.

- "the skill": « la compétence »

It's easy to remember, it's like "competency".

69. "accommodation": « un logement »

Example sentence

"Did you find proper accommodation near your new workplace?"

« As-tu trouvé un bon logement proche de ton nouveau lieu de travail ? »

Quick tip: accommodation

"accommodation" has no article in English, like "software". It's a collective noun, but you need an article in French. In French it's a quantifiable noun: « un logement », « deux logements » etc.

Breakdown

- "proper". That's a very idiomatic English word.

« bon » is a good translation: « un bon logement ».

« correct » is another one: « un logement correct ».

Notice how « correct » is placed after « logement », like most adjectives. However « bon » is actually placed before: « un bon logement ».

That's because it's a very common adjective like « grand » ("big"), or « vieux » ("old").

Grammar point: near

- "near": I chose to translate "near" with « proche ». I could have used « près »/« près de ».

"near" is « près de »; "close to" is « proche de ».

You may use both indiscriminately.

- "new": « nouveau »

The feminine is: « nouvelle ».

- "a workplace": « un lieu de travail ».

You should be familiar now with the way French deals with two nouns, using the genitive.

Hence "workplace" is « lieu **de** travail », literally "place of work".

70. "mergers/acquisitions": « les fusions acquisitions »

Example sentence

"Mergers and acquisitions is the busiest department in this consultancy firm."

« La direction des fusions-acquisitions est la plus active de cette agence de conseil. »

Quick tip: M&A slang

Here is a slang term for you. "M&A": « FUSACQ » (noun)

e.g. « la direction des fusacq ».

You may also use "M&A" in French as an acronym, in big international consultancy firms.

Breakdown

- "busy": « actif » or « occupé »

In this case « actif » is better. It's an adjective, so be careful to match it in gender and number with its noun.

- "the busiest": « la plus active »

It's also an adjective in the end, so you use « la plus active », because the noun it's matched with, is « la direction » (feminine).

- "**in** this consultancy firm": « **de** cette agence de conseil »

In English too, you could say "the business department **of** this consultancy firm".

But it's more common and more elegant to say "**in** this consultancy firm".

Be careful, sometimes the generic translations of prepositions don't apply.

- "a consultancy firm"/"a consulting firm": « une agence de conseil »/« une agence de consulting » (the latter only in an international business context).

71. "bankrupt": « en faillite »

Example sentence

"At this rate, the company will go bankrupt within a year."

« A ce rythme, l'entreprise fera faillite dans l'année. »

Breakdown

- "at this rate": « à ce rythme »

Be careful, there is a pronunciation trap here: « rythme » doesn't sound like "rhythm".

"th" sounds like « t » in French: "rhythm" =/= « rythme ».

- "will go": this is the future of "TO GO".

We use « fera faillite », the future of « FAIRE », instead of "TO GO".

Let's conjugate « FAIRE » in the future:

FAIRE – TO DO (future)

Je ferai	I will do
Tu feras	You will do
Il/Elle fera	He/She will do
Nous ferons	We will do
Vous ferez	You will do
Ils/Elles feront	They will do

- "the company will go": « l'entreprise ira/fera »
- "to go bankrupt": « faire faillite »
- "within": « en »/« dans »

"within a year": « dans l'année »

This is a set phrase here.

"a year" is « un an »/« une année ». "within a year" is translated as a set phrase: « dans l'année ».

Be careful here, "a" is an indefinite article but « l' » is a definite article.

It's one set phrase against another - "within a year": « dans l'année ».

72. "root cause": « une cause racine »

Example sentence

"We need to specify the root cause of last week's accident."

« Nous devons préciser la cause racine de l'accident de la semaine dernière. »

Breakdown

- "a root cause analysis": « une analyse de cause racine ».

This is exactly the same words but reversed. You will need this notion a lot, especially in a factory.

- "analysis": « une analyse »
- "a cause": « une cause »
- "a root": « une racine »

"a root cause analysis": « une analyse de cause racine »

Even the acronym is reverted - "RCA" becomes « ACR ».

The chart is called « un arbre des causes » (literally "a tree of causes"), as in a decision tree.

- "TO NEED": « DEVOIR »

This is an external obligation, you have to do this by law, you have to determine the cause of each accident.

- "an accident": « un accident »

It's transparent because it comes from Latin. Again, you don't need to know Latin, but it helps to be able to determine whether a word, in English or French or both, might have a Latin root, because it might be similar in both languages.

- "last week": « la semaine dernière »
- "a week": « une semaine »

- "last": « dernier » (masculine)/« dernière » (feminine).

73. "a day off": « un jour de congé »

Example sentence

"Why were you absent? Was it a business trip, sickness leave or a day off?"

« Pourquoi étiez-vous absent ? Etait-ce un déplacement professionnel, un congé maladie ou un jour de congé ? »

Breakdown

- « absent »: This word is transparent.
- "Was it...?": « Etait-ce... ?»

It's a question. Like in English, we invert the verb and the subject. "It was" becomes "Was it": « C'était » becomes « Etait-ce ».

- "a business trip": « un déplacement professionnel »

Now, a trip is usually « un voyage », and "business" is much more common and has a broader meaning in English than « professionnel ».

e.g. "Everything is business"; "Mind your own business".

In this case, it's a set phrase in French, a "business trip" is always « un déplacement professionnel ».

- "sickness leave": « un congé maladie »
- "to be sick": « être malade »
- "sickness": « la maladie »

e.g. "I'm sick to my stomach": « J'ai mal à l'estomac »

- "to be on leave": « PRENDRE un congé »
- "sickness leave": « un congé maladie »
- "a day off": « un jour de congé »

- "to take a day off": « PRENDRE un jour de congé »
- "to take several days off": « PRENDRE des (jours de) congés »

74. False friends

In these extra chapters we'll see some new words, some new expressions, specific technical vocabulary that will prove very useful in a business context.

So, this chapter will show you the most common false friends, also called "false cognates".

- For example, "TO ASSIST" is not « ASSISTER ». « ASSISTER » is "TO ATTEND".

e.g. "to attend a ceremony": « assister à une cérémonie »; "to attend a concert": « assister à un concert ».

"TO ASSIST" is « AIDER », e.g. "to assist someone" (as in "to help someone"): « aider quelqu'un ».

- "actually" is not « actuellement ». « actuellement » is "currently"; and "actually" is « en fait » (like "in fact").

This is a very common mistake among language learners.

- « une location » is not "a location". « une location » is "a rental". "a location" is « un endroit ».

- « PASSER un examen » is not "TO PASS an exam". « PASSER un examen » is "TO TAKE an exam".

"TO PASS an exam" is « RÉUSSIR à un examen ».

- "sensible" is not « sensible ». « sensible » is "sensitive"; and "sensible" is « judicieux ».

75. Software vocabulary

SOFTWARE VOCABULARY

Hardware	Le matériel informatique*
Software	Un logiciel
A file	Un fichier
The data	Les données**
A left click	Un clic gauche
A right click	Un clic droit
To copy-paste	Copier-coller
A folder	Un dossier
Microsoft Outlook	Microsoft Outlook
The Microsoft Office Suite	La suite Microsoft Office
Word	Word
Excel	Excel

*Careful, there is no article in English because it's a collective noun but we need one in French, « le matériel informatique ».

**It's also always plural in French - "the data": « les données ».

EXCEL/SPREADSHEET VOCABULARY

To insert	Insérer
A formula	Un formulaire
A cell	Une cellule
A row	Une rangée
A column	Une colonne

To save	Sauvegarder
An error	Une erreur
A sheet	Un tableau
A v-looker	Une recherche V
A screenshot	Une capture d'écran

SOFTWARE NAMES***

Powerpoint	Powerpoint
Photoshop	Photoshop
Lightroom	Lightroom
Hotmail	Hotmail
Access	Access
PDF	PDF
Facebook	Facebook
Google	Google
Twitter	Twitter
Instagram	Instagram

***Software names obviously stay the same. However, the pronunciation is different.

VISUALS

A pivot table	Un tableau croisé dynamique
A chart	Un graphique
A pie chart	Un camembert
A line chart	Un graphique linéaire
A bar chart	Un graphique en bâtons

A font	Une police
Bold	Gras
Italics	Italique
The spell check	Le correcteur orthographique
A space	Une espace****

****Be careful with this one, "space" as in "space conquest" is « un espace » ("space conquest" is « la conquête spatiale ». « l'espace » is masculine. However in IT, or on your keyboard, "a space" is « une espace » (feminine).

76. Private banking

PRIVATE BANKING

An account	Un compte
A bank	Une banque
An invoice	Une facture
A transfer	Un virement
An ATM	Un DAB (un distributeur automatique de billets)
A check	Un chèque
A teller	Un chargé d'accueil
A transaction	Une transaction
A direct debit	Un prélèvement automatique
A standing order	Un virement permanent
A receipt	Un reçu
To change money	Changer de l'argent
A currency	Une devise/une monnaie
A bill	Un billet
A coin	Une pièce
An online payment	Un paiement en ligne
A purchase order	Un bon de commande
Gross profit	Le profit brut
Net profit	Le profit net
The margin	La marge
EBITDA	L'EBITDA
The net present value	La valeur nette actuelle

(NPV)	
Capital expenditure	Les dépenses en capital
Operational expenditure	Les dépenses opérationnelles
Cash on delivery (COD)	Paiement à la livraison/Cash on delivery

77. Career and positions

CAREERS AND POSITIONS

A promotion	Une promotion
A transfer	Une mutation
To hire	Recruter
To fire	licencier
Team building	Le team building*
To integrate	Intégrer**
A manager	Un chef de service***
A business unit (BU)	Une business unit (BU)
The director of a business unit	Le directeur d'une business unit
The General Manager/CEO	Le Président-Directeur Général
A technician	Un technician
The EMEA director	Le directeur EMEA****
The financial director	Le directeur financier
The IT director	Le directeur des services informatiques (DSI)
The chief financial officer (CFO)	Le directeur financier
The chief financial and administrative officer (CFO)	Le directeur administratif et financier (DAF)
The chief technical officer (CTO)	Le directeur technique
The operations director	Le directeur des opérations

The manufacturing director	Le directeur de la production
The logistics expert	L'expert en logistique
The supervisor	Le chef d'équipe
The data analyst	L'analyste de données
The accountant	Le comptable
The senior counsel	Le conseiller juridique*****
The chairman of the board	Le président du conseil d'administration

*It's transparent because the whole team integration effort is very anglo and was picked up by the French.

**e.g. "to integrate a new team": « INTÉGRER une nouvelle équipe »

"a manager": « un chef de service »

***« manager » also exists but be careful when you use it. If you're addressing an audience that is not familiar with English be careful, use the French terms. Also « manager » can come across as being arrogant, because you're using an English term.

****In English you may also use "the **head** of a department" (instead of "director")

In French you only have « le directeur » (masculine)/« la directrice » (feminine).

*****"senior" is « senior » but it is only used in companies that have an international or anglo culture like consulting groups or multinationals

e.g. « quelqu'un de senior » ("a senior person"); « un poste senior » ("a senior position")

78. Acronyms

- "e.g." ("exempli gratia"): "ex." (« par exemple », as in "for example")
- "ETA": you can either use « ETA » as "estimated time of arrival" or « HPA », « heure prévue d'arrivée »
- "GDP" (Gross Domestic Product): « le PIB » (Produit Intérieur Brut)
- "department" can be shortened to "dept."; « direction » can be shortened to « dir. »
- "CC" in an email is the same: « CC »; "carbon copy" is « copie carbone »
- "BCC" is « CCI »; so "blind carbon copy" is « copie carbone invisible »
- "ASAP" is « ASAP » ("as soon as possible")
- "PP" as in "per procurationem", if you sign a letter or document on behalf of someone, is « PO » (« Pour Ordre »).

79. Sayings and metaphors

- "word of mouth": « le bouche à oreille »

So, the French literally says "the mouth to ear".

- "zero tolerance": « la tolérance zéro
- "by virtue of": « en vertu de »

This is legal jargon.

- "to strike while the iron is hot": « battre le fer tant qu'il est chaud »

This is exactly the same image from blacksmithing, but the word order is slightly different.

- "a vicious circle": « un cercle vicieux »
- "to be in the pipeline or in the works": « ÊTRE dans les tuyaux »

That means the task is being handled. The French literally says "it's in the pipes"

- "to bring a company to its knees": « METTRE une entreprise à genoux »
- "your wish is my command": « vos désirs sont des ordres »

The French says "your desires are orders"

- "to zero in on something": « se FOCALISER sur »

So, the English is originally a hunting saying.

But the French says "to focus on" simply, with no metaphor.

- "to put (something) on the back burner": « RELÉGUER (quelque chose) au second plan »

So, the English has a cooking or stove metaphor. The French has none and says "to push back to the background": « reléguer au second plan ».

Let's have some French sayings with their translations now.

- « ÊTRE sous l'eau »: "to be swamped"

Literally "to be underwater". It's a similar image.

- « une boîte »

That's a neutral slang term for "company."

For example, « je travaille dans la même boîte que mon père »: "I work in the same company as my father".

- « BOSSER »

That's a neutral slang term « TRAVAILLER ». For example, « je bosse dans cette boîte »: "I work in this company".

« boulot »/« taf » are neutral slang terms for « travail ».

e.g. « j'ai un bon boulot »/« J'ai un bon taf »: "I have a good job".

There is a verb version of « taf » which is « taffer ». It's a first group verb. It's like « travailler » and it conjugates the same way.

- « FAIRE d'une pierre deux coups »: "to kill two birds with one stone"
- « j'ai travaillé à la sueur de mon front »: "I worked my fingers to the bone"

The French literally says "my forehead was sweating from working"

- « je m'ennuie comme un rat mort »: "it's boring me to death"
- « je démissionne »: "I quit"

Final Words

Alright! So, this brings us to the end of this business French audiobook.

I really hope you've enjoyed it and learned some valuable and useful phrases, anecdotes and effective ways of communicating in a French environment. It's a big challenge to learn so many items, so the best results are to be gained by re-listening to the audiobook several times.

For rapid progress, use the audio book on repeat in your spare time, on the train or bus or when walking, on a daily basis. Repetition is key, and it really helps this material to become second nature. You can download it on bit.ly/businessfrenchbook or scan this QR code:

If you feel like the audiobook was a bit too advanced, and you need a refresher on French basics, check out my beginner audiobooks.

Again, if you find yourself in a tight spot and need urgent business translations, it would be my honor to give you expert, natural and contextually sound translations tailored to your specific industry and needs.

I love hearing from my listeners. Please let me know if you used any of the phrases you learned here in this audiobook.

If you enjoyed the book, please consider leaving us a review on the platform or site you made the purchase - this really helps us. Merci !

Printed in Great Britain
by Amazon